Bill and Margaret.

With all good wishes
and so many happy memories.

Murray.

An Unintentional Soldier

The Life of Murray Naylor

Rosa Naylor. Without whom much in this book would not have been achieved.

An Unintentional Soldier

The Life of Murray Naylor

Quacks Books

York

First published in Great Britain in 2018 by Quacks Books

isbn
hard back 978-1-912728-01-5

Set in twelve point Baskerville, justified with occasional text italicising with three point leading, headings ranged left and centred in eighteen point Baskerville bold, running heads centred in ten point italic. Page size 170mm x 245mm with a gutter margin of 15mm, head 25mm, for-edge 25mm and foot of 25mm, illustrated with photographs and scans, printed litho on a one hundred gsm book wove chosen for its sustainability, section sewn and hard back bound with green buckram cloth complete with a dust wrapper.

Page design by Katy Midgley

Published and printed by
Quacks Books
7 Grape Lane
Petergate
York Yo1 7hu
info@quacks.info
www.radiusonline.info
0044 (0)1904 635967

Contents

List of illustrations

Preface

This is a personal history and has been written so that my children and grandchildren, and indeed later generations and anyone outside the family should they be interested, will know what sort of life I have led and the consequences of the decisions I may have made during that time. It is not written to impress or prescribe, simply to set out the events of the last eighty years as experienced by me, while accepting that others may put a different interpretation on some of those events.

My story is written to the best of my recall. It is set down with a light touch and doesn't pull any punches where I feel that to be justified. I hope it will both interest and amuse; if it doesn't it will have failed in its purpose.

The title chosen for the book may mystify some. I never intended to follow a career as a soldier and it wasn't until towards the end of my two-year period of compulsory military service that I came to realise that the Army might provide the sort of professional employment I was seeking. Joining the Scots Guards to do National Service in 1956 was a major influence in my life. The regiment prepared me for and then steered me towards a full and satisfying professional career which generally gave me enormous pleasure and many lasting friendships. Everything which followed stemmed from there.

Murray Naylor

Summer 2018

Acknowledgements

I am grateful for the help and encouragement received in writing this personal history. Mrs Carol Trow has read and corrected the script on a number of occasions and has provided positive and sensible advice. Michael Sessions and his team at Quacks in York, in particular Katy Midgley, have taken a great interest in the book and have also offered wise guidance. Finally, Michael Scott, a regimental friend going back many years, has given good advice on matters relevant to the Scots Guards.

Royal Salute, Museum Gardens York 1988.
(L to R) David Wilson, Simon Price and Julian Browne.

Chapter One

Childhood and Ashton   1938 to 1950

The Beginning

I was born on 5 March 1938 at Eastham in the Wirral Peninsular not far from the southern bank of the river Mersey and close to the point where the Manchester Ship canal begins its thirty-six mile journey to connect the city of that name to the great seaport of Liverpool, once famously dubbed 'the second port of the Empire', at the mouth of the river. I recall nothing of the first years of my life although I later learnt that my father, Tom Naylor, born in July 1890, had married my mother, Dorothy Holt, in 1935, having previously been married to Quenelda Williamson in 1922 from whom he was later divorced in 1930. The wedding to my mother took place at St Columba's Church of Scotland, Pont Street, London. I believe that my parents were not permitted to marry in a Church of England church because my father had been divorced. Meanwhile my paternal grandfather, John Naylor, had died in 1906.

According to my father in a short history written not long before his death, the Naylors originated from South Lancashire in the late sixteenth century. The first recorded mention is of a John Naylor who was born at Croft near Winwick in 1589, in the reign of Queen Elizabeth I and not long after the defeat of the Spanish Armada. What employment those early Naylors undertook is unknown but they may well have been weavers using a loom in the family home. Another theory is that by virtue of their name they may have had a role in the construction or repair of church roofs. By the time of my arrival several centuries later the Naylors had gone up in the world having discovered the merits of high finance and banking, principally in Liverpool and surrounding Lancashire. My father had been educated at Eton, later going to Trinity College, Cambridge where he graduated in mechanical engineering and rowed for his college. Engineering always fascinated him and throughout his life he never missed an opportunity to practise the skills he learnt. It has always saddened me that I never inherited the same expertise although he did try to teach me. He served in the First World War in the Montgomeryshire Yeomanry in Egypt, Palestine and France but when peace came in 1918, rather than following a career as an engineer, he joined Sandbach Tinne & Company, a Liverpool sugar business managing the estates of the Demerara Company in British Guiana. He later became chairman of the company. During a long career in business, mainly in Liverpool, he was appointed Deputy Chairman of Martins Bank – subsequently subsumed by Barclays – and later Chairman of the Royal Insurance Company. He was highly respected in business circles in Liverpool when that city thrived as a centre of business and commerce in the 1950s and '60s before many well-established firms were merged or moved to London. He died in 1966 at the age of seventy-six.

My parents' wedding 1935.

My father had three brothers. Murray, the eldest who first lived at the family home at Leighton Hall near Welshpool before later moving to Angus in Scotland; Hugh who spent most of his life in East Africa, principally in Uganda, where he grew tea, and his twin brother Rowland who was killed at the battle of Festubert in Flanders in May 1915 while serving with the Royal Welch Fusiliers. All four brothers went to Eton so continuing a long Naylor tradition and all four served in the First World War. My Uncle Murray always struck me as rather aloof and I never felt that I really knew him. On the other hand, Uncle Hugh was good fun and on those occasions he paid a visit from Uganda, his arrival home was always enjoyed by his nephews and nieces. Neither Hugh nor Rowland married.

My mother was the youngest daughter of Richard and Eliza Holt and was born in June 1902. The Holts were Liverpool ship owners and my grandfather became the senior partner of Alfred Holt & Company which ran ships of the Ocean Steamship Company, popularly known as the Blue Funnel Line, from British ports principally to the Far East and Australasia. I must have met Grandfather Holt, who died when I was three, but never knowingly had a conversation with him. He was an important man in Liverpool and, in addition to managing the company's shipping business, for a period chaired the Mersey Docks and Harbour Board which administered the port. A Liberal in his politics he represented the Hexham parliamentary constituency in Northumberland from 1911 to 1918. I have always understood that he left politics in 1918 after a disagreement with Lloyd George, the war time Prime Minister and Liberal leader, over free trade, came to regret it and tried to find another seat but never succeeded. He was created a baronet in 1935 'for services to the port of Liverpool'. His wife, Eliza, was an American from New Jersey and as a result I am a mixture of English, Scottish and American ancestry, the Scottish link stemming from a connection on my father's side to the Murrays of Atholl, in Perthshire. My father contended that, if visiting Blair Castle and invited to sign the visitors book, a member of the family should always ask to sign the cousins' book! My mother used to say that when she married, the then Duke told my father that he would like to give them a wedding present; maybe thinking this might mean a gift of some land on the estate my father readily assented, only to be told that the Duke wished to give my mother 'the right to wear the Murray tartan.' My two sisters and later my own wife have in their turn assumed the same privilege!

My mother had two older sisters: Grace who married Anthony Methuen whose family owned Corsham Court near Bath, one of his illustrious ancestors being Field Marshal Lord Methuen, a soldier who came to prominence in the Boer War and who started his military life in the Scots Guards, the regiment my elder brother Christopher and I were later destined to join to undertake National Service; and Anne, a well read and erudite lady who was afflicted with acute deafness in her teens and who never married. Very courageously, she stood as a parliamentary candidate in Wavertree, a Liverpool inner city constituency, in the general election of 1945 thereby continuing the Holt Liberal political tradition. Unfortunately, she lost her deposit. She spent her final years in Scotland; always interesting and often provocative, she was not an easy person to communicate with, something her nephews and nieces used to play up to without compunction, but she was a kind and generous aunt, robust in her views and stimulating to talk with and I and my siblings have always had much to be grateful to her for. Many of the Holts were Unitarians.

Aunt Grace was a very understanding and competent person and rose to become national Treasurer of the Women's Institute after the war. Anthony, her husband, was an architect with firm views on matters like the positioning of early television aerials on houses. He disliked the spoiling effect they could have on a graceful building and for a long time allegedly forbade there to be one on the Ivy House in Corsham where Grace and he lived for much of their life together. Eventually an aerial was placed in the attic, but the picture was practically non-existent! They had three children and as our Methuen cousins we saw a bit of them, although I don't think any of us ever really got very close to them. They have all now died.

Meanwhile on the Naylor side of the family we had quite a group of first cousins, Uncle Murray having had four children by his first marriage and one by his second. Many are no longer alive – including Ian Pemberton, a cousin once removed, and his sister Gillian, who were closest in age to my siblings and me. Gillian's widowed husband, Tom Burr, remains a close friend to this day while a second set of cousins on Uncle Murray's side, the Burdis family, have grown nearer to us in recent years and happily we now see more of them than in the past.

Certain places were important to my parents, their ancestors and their contemporaries and some of them remain in the affections of later family generations to this day. Both the Naylors and the Holts lived at various times in different homes in the Liverpool area and Cheshire but it was Leighton Hall in mid Wales and Abernethy in the Highlands of Scotland, which probably commanded their deepest affections, although for very different reasons. I think my father never came to terms with the decision made by his elder brother, Murray, to sell Leighton in 1931 and to move to Scotland, while Abernethy, a Highland property in Inverness-shire owned by the Earls of Seafield was rented by the Holts on and off from the 1860s until my brother Christopher and I bought part of the estate in 1969 and owned it briefly until 1988.

I was never clear why my Uncle Murray should have sold Leighton but I suspect it was for financial reasons. Another possibility was that he once stood for election for the parliamentary seat of Welshpool as a Conservative but was defeated, not surprisingly since that part of central Wales was traditionally very Liberal. It needs to be remembered that, even as recently as the last century, some land owners saw a seat in Parliament almost as a right, particularly in more rural areas. Be that as it may, Uncle Murray's reasons for leaving Leighton must remain a matter of speculation. However, I am sure that, had my father ever had the chance of taking over the running of the estate, he would have relished it and, as a result, the lives of his children might have followed very different courses from those which they eventually took.

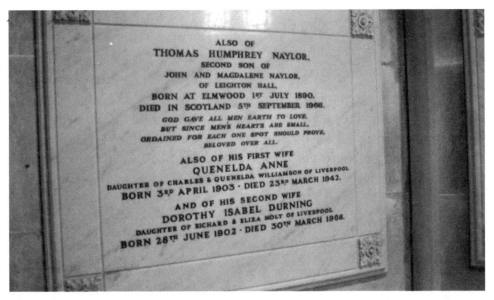

Memorial to my parents in Leighton Church Mausoleum.

In 1939, my parents decided to move from Eastham, probably to get further out from the increasingly expanding suburban communities around Liverpool, despite the longer commute that would mean for my father. They chose to live at the Grange in Ashton, a large house in spacious grounds to which they subsequently added a wing. The Grange was situated about eight miles from Chester, that ancient cathedral city whose origins stretch back to Roman times. I remember nothing of the move and have always marvelled at my parents' apparent confidence in undertaking such a step at a time when Europe was about to become enveloped in the second of two horrendous twentieth century world wars. The Grange was subsequently sold in 1969 when my mother moved to North Shropshire.

Back to Leighton. My great grandfather, John Naylor, inherited the estate in 1846 as a wedding present from a maternal uncle. Thereafter he built the present hall, redeveloped the farm, erected the church and constructed a bridge over the River Severn to provide a more direct link to Welshpool. John, his own son John, my grandfather, and Murray, his eldest grandson, lived there until 1931. The South East corner of the church is occupied by the Naylor Mausoleum, an almost completely detached octagonal building, which contains memorial plaques to nineteen members of the family dynasty although some recent deaths have not, as yet, been recorded. Meanwhile the churchyard contains seven Naylor graves including those of my parents.

Meanwhile, a large area of Inverness-shire stretching from the northern side of the Cairngorm Mountains towards the Moray Firth has, until fairly recently, been owned principally by the Seafield family. One of their properties – Abernethy, a few miles from Grantown on Spey – was first visited by Robert Holt, my maternal great grandfather, around 1860 following which the family went to the area on several occasions until Richard Holt took a long lease on the sporting estate in 1911. Since then the Holts and the Naylors have enjoyed Abernethy, either as tenants or owners, and still maintain a presence there although the current landholding is minimal by comparison with the past.

Abernethy.

Individual members of the family will have their own thoughts as to which of the two places described above means most to them. Leighton undoubtedly represents a period in the family's historic past but is now rarely visited although my brother, Christopher, who lives reasonably close, keeps an eye on the family graves. Meanwhile Abernethy was always central to my parents' lives and also to those of Christopher, me and my two sisters and now to those of our children and, I suspect, increasingly our grandchildren. In addition, the families of my brother and I still occupy a house on the former estate.

Ashton

The Grange was an ideal place for a young family to grow up. Set in undulating wooded countryside – untypical of Cheshire which in general is rather a flat county – the house and its numerous outbuildings and spacious garden afforded countless opportunities for play and the pursuit of rural pastimes. Christopher, born in 1936, me and my two sisters – Carolyn born in

The Grange.

1940 and Mary Anne in 1941 – all made the most of it, although, unlike them, I never embraced the many opportunities to learn to ride. Indeed, they all became rather good at various facets of equestrian sports including hunting, dressage and, in Mary Anne's case, point to point racing. Their love of the horse wasn't surprising given that my parents both rode and hunted until the war but it was not for me and I tended to do my 'own thing', my inability to relate to the horse quite understandably tending to set me apart from my siblings. If I recall, I fell off one of the ponies at an early age and caught mumps shortly afterwards. The two events were of course unconnected, except in my mind!

While the Grange was an appropriate house for a growing family, to begin with wartime conditions imposed restrictions on what we might do: petrol was rationed, orange juice, specifically for younger children, was dished out from time to time at the village hall, other necessities were controlled by ration book, while evacuees from nearby cities came to live with us for a time and my father once again donned military uniform, this time to command the local Home Guard platoon. I was too young to fully understand all these events and indeed the significance of Dunkirk, the succession of defeats inflicted upon Britain from 1940 to 1942, the loss of Singapore, the triumph of Alamein, the landings in Italy and Normandy and eventual victory over Germany and four months later Japan. However, living where we did we experienced at a distance some of the trauma inflicted upon cities like Liverpool and Birkenhead which were regularly bombed in the blitz. I recall one morning waking up to find the lawn at Ashton covered in burnt paper following a particularly heavy German raid on Merseyside.

However, one incident has always stuck in my memory. It must have been in late 1943 or early 1944 after the Germans had successfully developed their V1 and V2 rockets as weapons of mass destruction to be fired indiscriminately at centres of population. Christopher and I shared a room at the time and early one Sunday morning in summer, unable to sleep and having constructed 'wigwams' out of our bedclothes, we suddenly became aware of a blue flash in the sky emitting a sound like an aircraft which, at almost the moment we became aware of it, cut out. Of course, the latter was the prelude to the rocket dropping from the sky although, in our naivety, we speculated as to what it might mean. These musings were shattered seconds later when the V2 crashed in a field about two miles away near the Chester road killing a horse but otherwise doing no damage. Ashton was on the flight path to Liverpool and the rocket meant for that city. Two little boys demolished their 'wigwams' very quickly!

I also remember being bitterly disappointed on VE day in May 1945 when I was not allowed to stay up late to see an effigy of Hitler being burnt on the top of a bonfire. We had all helped to build the pyre in the sandpit near the Grange earlier in the day. On another occasion after the end of the war a light aircraft got into difficulties and crashed in the wood close to the Grange when Carolyn and I were standing on the lawn. Nobody was hurt – the pilot having bailed out – but the starkness of the incident gave us both nightmares for a long time.

My parents employed a group of people who worked at the Grange and whom we got to know well and enjoy. Frank Davies, the groom who was doubtless responsible for teaching the girls much about horsemanship: Walter Buck, the rather humourless gardener and Tom Ridgeway, the assistant gardener, able to turn his hand to sorting out most problems, all became good friends. I used to look upon Tom as a real buddy despite the difference in age and we spent many a happy hour discussing life, ferreting, pigeon shooting, making bonfires, cleaning out the septic tank or cutting wood. The freedom allowed us at Ashton was a privilege, our parents seemingly being very aware of the need to give growing children space and practical experience of life from an early age. They trusted us and I don't think we ever betrayed that trust, or not often.

Meanwhile, in the house, my parents had quite a retinue of people who came to help run things and look after us children. Nannie King (although that only became her name on marrying in the early fifties after she left) looked after us and kept us in order. Never flustered and only rarely admonitory, she quietly steered us in the right direction supporting my mother in coping with four children. A down to earth and sensible woman originally from Rotherham in South Yorkshire, we missed Rhoda King greatly when she left my mother's employment. Following her came Nanny Evans or Nig Nag as she was known. Another stalwart supporter of us children she mainly looked after my two sisters although we all benefitted from her being with us. At one stage we also had a governess, 'Bunny' Haire who came from Dublin, and I remember

Christopher and I doing lessons in the 'school room'. Using the same room my mother at another time employed a former wartime land girl to teach me the piano, a hopeless task as they both soon learnt. I think she was called Jean Day and to this day I wish she had persevered.

Besides the nannies, there were others who came and went including a bevy of Italians who arrived from war torn Italy around 1950 to seek domestic employment in Britain. I can recall Theresa and later Rosa but there were others. They all helped the family and we kept in touch with them long after they left. But the star of them all was Edith Westley who retired in the late 1950s, although after that she kept on returning to help my mother. She was diminutive in stature but a bundle of energy and had been with my father's family since the turn of the century when she had helped to bring him up. We loved her and she loved all of us, in particular my parents' four dogs who were left in her charge when they were absent, whereupon they would often sleep on her bed and she on the floor! Edith never married and eventually settled at her family's home in Woolton, Liverpool not far from where some of my father's relatives had lived. She was the salt of the earth.

My father. High Sheriff of Cheshire 1950/1.

We all adored my mother and had appropriate respect for my father. Both born towards the end of the Victorian era, their attitude to raising a family was not unexpectedly different from the conventions of today's world. We were kept on quite a tight rein, disciplined to be part of a family team and expected to conform without question to the social criteria applying at the time; we lived in an atmosphere where the notion of family was paramount. It might therefore seem ungrateful to criticise how one was brought up by one's parents but in retrospect I wish that I had been allowed greater latitude to be myself. I often felt there were certain aspects of life I was never encouraged to learn about, maybe subjects best avoided; whether that was due to diffidence, particularly on my father's part, it was in a way strange because he could be very relaxed, possessed a nice sense of humour and enjoyed practical jokes although not always so keen when played on him! He also went out of his way to involve us in activities of a practical nature when, using his mechanical skills, he would teach us the rudiments of how to do tasks around the place. One of his best initiatives was to introduce Christopher and me to the world of commerce and business by arranging visits to local enterprises so that we could see for ourselves the contribution they made to society. The shipyards in Birkenhead, a Blue Funnel boat, a cotton mill in Bolton, the salt mine at Northwich and the Edgehill railway depot in Liverpool were all on the agenda. But he was undoubtedly a man of austere beliefs and, although he denied us little to prepare us for our future lives, we grew up in his image. I suppose he was so absorbed in ensuring that Christopher and I should mirror his Victorian characteristics that he really didn't stop to consider how the world we were about to enter, might not necessarily be the same as the one he had been brought up in fifty years earlier.

Another example of my father's imagination was his involvement in amateur aviation. Although he ceased flying before I was born he and his first wife, both amateur pilots, used to fly light aircraft during their eight years together and they competed in several competitions. Indeed, my father won the Liverpool – Manchester Air Race on two occasions. He used to tell an amusing story of how when he was looking for a prep school for my half-brother, Peter, he telephoned the headmaster of Stone House School in Kent to inform him that he wished to fly down from Liverpool to visit his school to assess its suitability. Asking where he might land his Tiger Moth aircraft, he was assured that he could put down on the school playing fields which would be clearly marked. Trusting in this advice my father set off arriving overhead where he thought the school might be to find the letters 'Stone House' laid out on the playing fields indicating where he should put down which he duly did; his confident approach was unusual enough but, even more bizarre was the fact that when his aircraft landed it blew all the boys' caps, laid out to spell the school's name, into the surrounding bushes and back gardens, never to be recovered, much to the chagrin of parents! Peter was not enrolled in the school.

My mother was his great support throughout their life together, as loyal and understanding a wife as anybody could reasonably be blessed with. She sustained us all, encouraging and shielding us, ultimately enjoying the reward of seeing us all go out into the wider world to carry the family banner. Few families could have been as lucky as we were.

My mother. With her dogs sitting on the air raid shelter at Ashton.

My parents chose four people to be my godparents whose responsibility I suppose was to ensure 'I learnt my catechism' and was properly guided in the ways of the Christian faith from an early age. I am not sure that any of the four really fulfilled their responsibilities and one, Major General Jimmy Harrison, died not long after my birth. The others were Jack Hobhouse, a forbidding rather frightening man who was a senior manager of Blue Funnel Line, Ba Dewhurst, good fun and quite feisty, and Joan Brooks whose husband farmed near Chipping Norton, to where I wrote on countless occasions to thank for presents but which place I can't recall at all! I am sure that in their different ways they all helped to nurture me.

In 2013, I happened to be visiting a publishing firm in Barnsley in South Yorkshire and, while waiting to meet my appointment, I noticed a plaque on the wall stating that the building I was in had been part of a Territorial Army drill hall before conversion to its present use. The plaque recorded the opening of the drill hall by a Major General J.M.R. Harrison of the Royal Artillery in 1938. Having never knowingly met Jimmy Harrison in real life, I felt that that oversight had been corrected even if it had taken over seventy-five years!

As already said I was rather the odd one out at Ashton, pursuing separate interests to my siblings, although some were shared with Christopher. From as far back as I can recall I was always intrigued by anything to do with railways, an interest which has remained with me all my life. Their purpose and how they worked fascinated me. At quite an early stage my father asked me the usual parental question 'what might I want to do when I left school', a question I answered not by saying 'to be an engine driver' but rather that I would like to work in railway management. My father who, like so many of his generation, had a firm dislike of the post war Labour government's nationalisation policies, indicated that this would be a bad move, a put down which he got Godfather Jack Hobhouse to endorse later. Suitably chastened, the prospect of doing something that I thought I might actually enjoy, evaporated. I have often wondered how life would have proceeded if I had persisted.

However, the interest remained, and I spent much holiday time bicycling to watch trains and photographing them. That might strike a reader as rather dismal, but I enjoyed my own company, although when my father – himself quite absorbed by trains – would suggest he accompany me on an expedition it would be a red-letter day, especially if we ended up placing pennies on the railway line to watch a passing locomotive flatten them! Once asked by our parents where we might like to spend the last Sunday of one summer holidays before return to school, Christopher and I replied in unison that we would enjoy a day spent on Crewe station, a proposal however unwelcome to my mother. A compromise was subsequently reached, and we enjoyed a picnic watching trains passing on the West Coast mainline south of the station. I think my father was rather pleased, the more so when he later discovered a large, perfectly formed square of coal stamped with the 'Midland Railway' insignia, amongst the lineside brambles which we rather laboriously lugged back to the car and put in the boot to be later burnt, almost ritually, on the drawing room fire at Ashton. My mother was however less amused by the day.

The other member of the family who shared my railway interest was Peter. He was our half-brother being the only child of my father's first marriage. Born in 1923 he too had been educated at Eton after which he had enlisted in the RAF for the last two years of the war piloting Sunderland flying boats on Atlantic anti-submarine patrols. My early recollection was always of a dashing figure in light blue uniform, service cap at a jaunty angle, often seen with a pipe stuck in his mouth, a pose traditionally adopted by many of his Air Force colleagues. He was a bit of a hero to my generation, full of fun and interested in all that we did and able to relate to us in a way in which our parents maybe didn't always. I spent many a happy hour discussing railways with him and after he married and had a house near Lake Windermere, we would go on expeditions to watch the mighty LMSR steam locomotives thundering up Shap Bank on their way to Scotland.

Peter.

In 1946, he married Paddy Illingworth whose family divided their time between Ilkley in Yorkshire and Far Sawrey in the Lake District, where Peter eventually took over the running of the Bryerswood Estate. Peter became involved and active in many aspects of Cumbrian life. Prior to moving to live full time in the Lakes, he had worked in Liverpool for Demerara Company eventually following my father as Chairman until the company was taken over in the 1970s. The take over of Demerara Company was one of the earliest examples of a business led absorption of a commercial company by a City financier intent upon stripping out the profitable parts of a business without thought for the staff, then disposing of the rest. I think Peter was very hurt by the occurrence and the way it happened. Paddy died in 2013 but Peter, now aged ninety-four, still goes strong. He and I were always quite close despite differences in age and of late we have become even closer. He remains a stalwart brother or uncle to us all.

An Anglo-Scottish express passing through the Lake District.

I might say that Peter was always fulsome in his gratitude to my mother for the fact that she went out of her way to involve him fully with the family when she married my father. Although he never says so, I think his early years as an only child in a possibly less than happy home, spending much of his time with Nannie, must have taken its toll; that he eventually turned out the person he did, says much for my mother and her inclusive support as well as for his own resilient personality.

Life at Ashton was quite social, my parents having many local Cheshire friends while my mother had cousins and a number of more distant relatives living in and around Liverpool, with others in North Wales. There always seemed to be somebody staying at the Grange or coming to lunch and my mother enjoyed the company of people and being able to entertain. She was a kind and generous person with a strong sense of family and heritage. Equally my father had a strong sense of right and wrong being highly principled and supportive of others, particularly if they had a problem. Maybe, as I have suggested, he was sometimes harder on us four children than may have been warranted but then that is a parental tendency and I don't think we are any the worse for it. Both my parents were what I suppose would be termed 'god fearing' people with church on a Sunday never missed unless there was a good reason. Many is the long and often tedious sermon, preached by the Rev Edward Barnes, we sat through in Ashton Heyes Church but his exhortations clearly made an impression since I have remained a committed churchman ever since those days. As I shall reiterate later, my early grounding as a practising Christian has always remained with me and I have no doubt that it supplied me with that moral stimulus so necessary in life if a person is to be both kind and realistic in the way they lead their lives and influence others.

As well as their involvement in the life of the county both my parents shot, fished and stalked; my father was a fine marksman and my mother a very capable shot with a 16 bore gun until well into her seventies. As a consequence, all four of us children were taught to shoot and had ample opportunity to perfect our skills at Abernethy, where we walked the moors in line with our parents looking for grouse. We were very fortunate to have such opportunities. At one stage before she married my father, my mother held the record for catching the largest salmon on the river Spey.

As a family we usually took holidays in Scotland; we either motored to Abernethy or travelled overnight by sleeper from Crewe to Aviemore. On one occasion it was just my father and myself who went by train and, as was his custom, he was intent on travelling First Class in a single birth compartment. Since he was not inclined to pay for a second birth for me he decided he would rig up a hammock for me but his 'lash up' did not survive once the train picked up speed and, much to his annoyance, we had to share his bunk! I might say Christopher and I always loved travelling overnight to Scotland on the sleeper, a form of transport which for us generated excitement at every stage of the journey despite the discomfort of the early trains with their basic four berth compartments and minimal bedding.

We didn't travel abroad for holidays after the war, principally because visits overseas were then not very fashionable or indeed practicable for reasons of currency restrictions. The first time I went abroad was in 1951 when my parents took Christopher and me by car for a week staying near Tours on the Loire river in order to visit the French chateaux in the area. I remember being amazed at seeing the car being put on a sort of wooden and iron frame and then swung onto the ferry at Dover; there were no roll on roll off ships in those days. I also recall being upbraided by my father for falling asleep on the journey and for not taking an interest in the interminably dull French countryside we passed through in the Pas de Calais.

Loading the car at Dover.

1953 was the year of the Coronation and Christopher and I went with my parents to watch the procession returning from Westminster Abbey, from the offices of Martins Bank close to Trafalgar Square. Sadly, the day was marred by rain, but it was made for us when the carriage carrying Queen Salote of Tonga, a British dependency in the South Pacific, came to a halt opposite where we were. The queen was a very large lady and was accompanied by a diminutive man whom it was popularly thought to be her next meal!

Overall, I think my parents fitted well into Cheshire and the wider social scene and were both highly respected. They had a host of friends and were popular. They gave us all a great start in life.

Fourth of June 1956. Hibernia. DMN 2.

Chapter Two

Growing up

School Days

Generally speaking, I never enjoyed school. There is probably nothing very remarkable in that since lots of children have found the shock of leaving home and being introduced to a disciplinary routine not previously experienced, at best disconcerting, at worst traumatising. In fact, my first school was the Abbey day school in Chester close to the cathedral. I cannot recall anything about my sojourn there, but I think I probably enjoyed it because Christopher and I used to travel each day on a train from Mouldsworth, the local station for Ashton, to Northgate station in the city. I cannot imagine I learnt much.

By train to school.

With Nicholas Swinton on an outing.

Gardening at Selwyn House.

At eight, I was sent away to board at Selwyn House, a prep school at Broadstairs in Thanet. The school was run by a couple called John and Joan Green; he was tall and thin and she very large. One of a number of schools in an area close to the sea it was assumed that such a location would be good for our health, although I don't think that it was the only reason why it was selected for Christopher and me. I have always believed that my parents had connections with the school which had been evacuated to North Wales during the war to escape the risk of bombing in Kent, and maybe they overlooked the fact that it would return there once hostilities ended. Broadstairs was not a convenient place to reach although a through train from Chester to Margate avoiding London made for an easy journey at the beginning and end of term. Coastal holiday resorts are never scintillating places and in the depths of winter can be positively awful; I still have unhappy memories of those occasional week ends when my parents did visit, staying at Mrs Lobb's guest house or in the almost empty Grand Hotel in November, an enormous draughty edifice at one end of Broadstairs bay, which smelt of cooked cabbages. Not surprising really since Thanet is renowned for growing cabbages and cauliflowers!

I can remember little of my time at prep school other than that I won a prize for the best garden – no doubt with others – and another for Divinity which still surprises me. I made some friends, a few of whom – Nicholas Swinton, Tim O'Connor Fenton and Alwyn Dudley Smith – have reappeared in my life since we came to live in Yorkshire, but I was not sorry to leave in 1951 having scraped into the very bottom form at Eton. What would have been my parents' contingency plan had I not done so, I have no idea. Selwyn House gave me my first experience of exercising authority, an area in which I failed lamentably when as the monitor responsible for the Third dormitory, I allowed some boys to leave the school one night using a fire escape; John Green was very angry!

Eton was of course a totally different prospect. Christopher preceded me there by two years and for a time we shared a room in George Tait's Boys House or 'Tutors', an unusual arrangement and doubtless tiresome for him but probably necessitated by overcrowding. George Tait was a remarkable man. A teacher of Latin and Greek and an expert on Greek history, he struck me on first meeting as coming from another universe which maybe was unsurprising since I understood little of such subjects! He was quite eccentric – greeting all those he met when riding his outsize bicycle down Eton's thoroughfares or along the river Thames towpath when coaching a house rowing team, with a cheery cry of "Hullo, Old You" – but nonetheless I think he knew what was going on and generally ran a good and happy house.

Eton was in those days run on federal lines; each house master or house tutor as he was known jealously guarded their right to have responsibility for overseeing and, if required, adjusting the aspirations of the fifty or sixty boys placed in their charge. Years afterwards reading the correspondence which passed between George and my father about my progress or lack of it, it is absolutely clear that my house tutor was the key influence in steering me through five years at the school. The Headmaster or 'Headman' as he was irreverently known – Dr Robert Birley during my time – never entered the lives of most boys unless they were either very clever or very naughty when they might be sent to see him to receive appropriate congratulations or punishment. Birley was not everybody's favourite headmaster but he was a strong leader and managed to control his housemasters, something which some of his successors did not, with unfortunate consequences. When I was there the school had around 1100 pupils (I think it is probably twice that number now) so there needed to be a degree of delegation. While Eton will always be criticised for providing elitist schooling for those whose parents can afford it, schemes to include children from less fortunate families have long been provided and are being expanded all the time. However, the debate over whether to permit the continued existence of fee paying schools when the maintained sector is striving to improve and, indeed in many respects is doing so, will continue as long as politicians have the breath to make the opposing ideological arguments; those arguments are usually more about equal opportunity and the provision of a single Government run system rather than the provision of some centres of excellence which can and indeed do, usefully support and supplement state provision, without placing undue pressure on the public finances.

In retrospect, I suspect I didn't really deserve to go to Eton because I did not make the most of the opportunities offered. I scraped in, achieving pitifully low marks in the Common Entrance Exam and thereafter shone neither academically nor on the sports field. I was never given a position of authority with the exception of being promoted to the rank of corporal in the CCF, an extra-mural activity which boys joined voluntarily under pressure to do so! In time I made my way into the Upper School and when the opportunity came, specialised in History, a subject which I have always enjoyed. One of the great benefits of that decision was that the specialist tutor whose pupillage I joined was Willie Gladstone, a then unmarried master or 'beak' in the Eton vernacular and the great grandson of W.E. Gladstone, four times Queen Victoria's Prime Minister between 1868 and 1894. Willie was a lovely man, interesting, very approachable and a good teacher; had I thought about it at the time he was the sort of person I would have liked to grow up to emulate. After Eton he went on to become headmaster at Lancing College in West Sussex, later being appointed as the Chief Scout, and until his recent death lived at Hawarden Castle in North Wales. He prompted my enjoyment of history and for that I shall always be grateful.

I fared little better at games. Most of the usual sports passed me by but, like all Etonians, in the winter months I played the Eton Field Game. The latter was a mixture of soccer and rugby, the ball sometimes being kicked or dribbled, the players sometimes confronting each other in a scrum or bully similar to that on a rugby pitch; I rather enjoyed the game but showed only the rawest of skills until my last winter when I was selected to captain M'Tutors house second eleven or Sine (those without) and we won the inter house competition. It was possibly my proudest moment at Eton!

GAD Tait's house four in the Eton 'bumping races' 1956. Cox: Russell. Stroke: David Murray-Threipland 3: DMN. 2: Micheal Rena. Bow: David Thomson.

I also rowed during the summer term or 'half' as it was known. Sculling up the Thames to Maidenhead or on occasions even as far as Marlow was a wonderful way to use free time when there was a school holiday. Again, in my last year I rowed in my House four in the May bumping races, held over four evenings when houses attempted to bump their way to the 'Head of the River' by catching up and bumping the boat in front. I can't recall how we did in 1956 but, coached by George Tait, we made reasonable progress. A few weeks later on that great Eton holiday, the Fourth of June, held every year to commemorate the birthday of George III who established a close rapport with the school during the course of his long reign, I was selected to row in the *Hibernia* eight in the procession of boats and received my Lower Boats cap as a result. I might say this was the only cap I received while at Eton. The procession of boats took place on the evening of the Fourth down river from the main part of the school at Fellows' Eyot where parents, staff, girlfriends and sundry others came to spectate. Crews in each of the dozen or so boats in the procession had to stop rowing when they passed the onlookers, stand up, take their oars out of the water and hold them vertically in front of them while at the same time doffing their straw boaters. It was a hazardous exercise at the best of times but late on into an evening of celebration and revelry there were inevitable swampings with crews ending up in the river. I don't recall anybody ever being drowned but I suppose it could have happened.

In 1956, I sat the School Certificate exam, the ultimate test of any academic success at Eton and achieved five passes – not a great record but equally not a disgrace. Prior to the exam my father had been in consultation with George Tait over the prospect of my attending university to complete my preparation for the wide world yonder. There were several obstacles to such a possibility, notably my weak academic record, the exam which I would need to pass and the fact that I would have to undertake two years National Service before I could go to whichever university might accept me. My father thought only in terms of Oxbridge which was a pity since, as I am sure George knew, there was little possibility of either of those universities accepting me and the chances of passing their entrance examinations fairly remote. Needless to say, I was not really privy to the discussions; in retrospect I was saddened by the fact that nobody thought of looking further than Oxbridge at some of the very good universities in those days labelled as 'redbricks' such as Exeter or Edinburgh. Of course, there would have been no guarantee I would have got into any of them either but it must have been worth a try. I think that I would have benefitted, especially if I had read History or Geography, the two subjects which I always enjoyed most and which I still enjoy to this day. I also believe I would have been a much better and more rounded individual had I had the experience of a tertiary education.

I made some good friends at Tait's, some of whom have remained in contact ever since; Christopher Clayton in particular – probably my oldest chum outside my immediate family – while Mervyn Blakeney, Ben Thompson McCausland and Peter Lewis were others.

Passing out at Eaton Hall OCS July 1957. The Princess Royal the inspecting officer.

National Service

I think it was the complications posed by the need to undertake National Service which finally scuppered any attempt to try for university. The requirement to serve two years in the armed services after leaving school around the age of eighteen was not discontinued until 1959 so, after leaving Eton in July 1956, I reported to the Guards Depot at Caterham in Surrey on 12th September for basic training. The initial few weeks proved quite a shock to the system as we were chased hither and thither around the barracks by seemingly ferocious non-commissioned officers apparently intent on destroying us. We gradually had all the lethargy knocked out of our systems and became much fitter and, as was intended, a lot more disciplined and less cocksure. While I probably didn't understand at the time, the purpose of the rough treatment meted out was to reduce us to basic individuals and, when shorn of all our misconceptions and prejudices, to build us up again into potential soldiers who would do the

Army's bidding without argument or complaint. It was very effective. Many of my fellow recruits became good friends and I still see some of them quite regularly, in particular Christopher Clayton, already mentioned above, who was going to the Life Guards and Thomas Boyd-Carpenter who was also destined for the Scots Guards. John Purves was another and he later became an MEP in Scotland. In our hut at Caterham I slept next to a chap called John Manassei, an Italian Count who for some reason was to do his National Service in the regiment. A formidable but very capable Sergeant called 'Spud' Thomson was our squad instructor and a guardsman – Ted Aldred – lived in our hut and imposed a rigid discipline on us at all times. Both were Scots Guardsmen, and both became good friends when I later joined the regiment. Aldred eventually became Head of the CID in Liverpool, a great accolade for him and indeed the regiment.

Since 1959, the question of the reinstatement of National Service has often been mooted, not necessarily as a way of training people for the armed forces but rather as a means of dragooning some of the country's feckless youth into learning discipline, commitment and standards. An attractive idea in principal but I doubt it would ever work; the services would not have welcomed it since the presence of conscripts would have hindered the increasingly rapid technical development of war fighting and training, while the nation, experiencing ever growing standards of living, would probably have baulked at a return to the disruption and restrictions imposed when conscription really was seen to be justified

In November, we were all put through the War Office Selection Board or WOSB to see if we were ready to go on to the next stage of training at the Eaton Hall Officer Cadet School near Chester. Not surprisingly given my hitherto lack of academic success and self-confidence, I failed the test along with about twenty others and had to re-sit it a few months later. After a second attempt, I and a dozen others followed our former colleagues to Cheshire to the Duke of Westminster's country home which housed the cadet school, where we undertook weapon and field training until July 1957 when I passed out to be commissioned as 2nd Lieutenant Naylor in the Scots Guards. I enjoyed Eaton Hall and found the training to be stimulating and pitched less narrowly than that at Caterham. In addition, the fact that I was only a dozen miles from Ashton and home and, by that time had my own car – a

Morris 8 Series E, number GMA998 – made frequent trips to the Grange to reacquaint myself with 'civilisation' and reasonable meals, possible and a welcome benefit!

Looking back over my time at school and my first year in the Army I must say that I owe much to George Tait at Eton. A tireless support to all those who passed through his hands during his stewardship of Warre House, he was a most humane and understanding man who took immense trouble to get things right for those for whom he had responsibility; in the main he left his charges the better for their being guided by him. He died many years ago, but he will always remain in my affections as somebody who guided me wisely, with great consideration and human kindness. Like many of Eton's finest he left an indelible mark on the school and boys alike.

The decision to serve my two-year period of compulsory service in the Scots Guards was really taken by my father. I suspect he felt that I had too little knowledge of the options to decide such a matter for myself and he was right. He had good friends in the regiment and he therefore consulted them, having doubtless also talked to them earlier about brother Christopher, who had joined up for his two years in the Army in 1954. General Claude Dunbar and Colonel Henry Clowes were both men of wisdom and experience and in time I came to know both well and appreciate their support. All this was very different from what happens now when potential officer recruits invariably decide their choice of regiment for themselves and, once they arrive at Sandhurst, are often lobbied by other regiments keen to persuade them to change their minds and sign up with them. Meanwhile my father's decision to steer me towards the Scots Guards, given our family background, was logical and, as it turned out, very fortuitous.

12 September 1956 was I suppose the date I ceased to be a child and embarked upon the road to becoming an adult. I had crossed a line and although I don't think I fully realised it at the time, my passage through life was from thereon pretty well laid out before me. I was to undertake tasks, visit places, meet people and enter into commitments I couldn't possibly have envisaged at the time; luckily, I was to grow in confidence to meet the challenges which lay ahead. There would be plenty of them.

On patrol in the Oman 1961.

Chapter Three

A Scots Guardsman
1958 to 1979

1958 to 1960

The next twenty-two years of my life were spent mostly at regimental duty serving principally in the 2nd Battalion of the Scots Guards with one tour in the 1st Battalion, or at extra regimental duty. Because the routine of life in a battalion varies little and then only depending upon where the latter is based, and the operational role allotted to it, in this section I have only highlighted those places and events I feel to be of most interest.

My introduction to battalion life passed without undue problems. I reported to the 2nd Battalion, commanded at the time by Colonel Michael Fitzalan Howard, at Chelsea Barracks and was posted to the Right Flank (Company) under the leadership of Major George Nickerson. Fellow young officers in the company were Simon Barrow and David Baird-Smith. I was entrusted with command of No 2 Platoon and had Sergeant Sanderson to guide me over my early months. Our role was public duties guarding the Royal palaces, the Tower of London and at night the Bank of England. It was all rather heady stuff after the rigours of basic infantry training and not very demanding on one's time, leaving plenty of scope to enjoy the social life of London.

George was a charming if somewhat old-fashioned officer. He had served during the last years of the war and his instincts led him to do things in a traditional and at times rather unimaginative way, not that the routine of providing soldiers for royal duties allowed much scope for exciting alternatives. Chelsea Barracks was a depressing place – later demolished and rebuilt in a more modern if unattractive style in the 1960s – and we all tried to spend as little time as possible within its walls. Escape to the outside world was easy and apart from looking after my platoon of thirty men and doing my share of public duties, there was little to keep me there. I initially lived in the Officers Mess but after a while Simon Barrow and I moved out to share a room in a house in Royal Avenue, just off the King's Road. It was owned by a Miss Medlicott who had rather an unpleasant chow which one had to ward off as one went up the stairs. The house was demolished some years ago.

The Bank Piquet.

Public duties required considerable preparation and although they generated much external interest and the various Guards did have a security role, they palled after a while. As with all such tasks some people enjoyed the rather Gilbert and Sullivan like life and couldn't wait to do another tour, while others took any opportunity to be posted elsewhere when a tour loomed. The principal duties are well known, many still being undertaken today, but the one task which has not survived is the Bank of England Piquet which marched each evening from Chelsea Barracks to the Bank in the City to guard the vaults; there the guardsmen would stand sentry while the officer was provided with dinner and a decanter of port by the bank staff! It was a long march and the passage of the piquet escorted by a mounted policeman and preceded by a piper, helped to further disrupt the already disrupted London traffic. It was often alleged that, if it came on to rain, rather than stopping to put on capes, the officer in command might order the guardsmen to march into the nearest Underground station and complete the rest of the journey by tube train! An apocryphal story or maybe not?

Of course, there was more to public duties in London than the daily guards mounted from either Chelsea or Wellington Barracks. The Queen's Birthday Parade, guards of honour for visiting state dignitaries and special occasions like the State Opening of Parliament all appeared at some stage in the annual programme. In 1958 the battalion left Chelsea moving first to Shorncliffe near Folkestone and later to Assaye Barracks, Tidworth to join 1st Guards Brigade, at the time part of the UK Strategic Reserve. It was a relief to get out of London and to start training as a battalion, although we still managed to return to the capital for social events, nightly travelling the eighty miles there and back before the days of motorways in order to be on parade at 7.45am the next morning! Tony Boam, a very efficient officer, was Adjutant and it simply wasn't worth risking not returning in time. A punishment of twenty-eight days as duty officer was not to be recommended. Incidentally it was in those days possible to book a bed in a dormitory at the former Guards Club in Charles Street for ten shillings a night; the only snag was that one could often find someone else in the bed you thought you had booked!

One of the Anti-Tank platoon's guns and 3 man detachment 1957.

Colonel Adrian Seymour took over command before we left London and I was moved to Support Company to become the Anti-Tank platoon commander with Major Tony Harrison as my immediate superior. Sergeant Walker was my platoon sergeant and John Whiteley and Anthony Innes commanded the Mortar and the Machine Gun platoons respectively. Tony was the most delightful man, a bachelor with a lovely dry sense of humour, a master of the ready comment. As the supposed experts in our various weapon systems we platoon commanders were left alone to get on with training our teams and the independence we had was very welcome. It was a happy company and it was sad when it was broken up in order that the battalion could undertake a military trial designed to produce a more efficient organisational structure called the 774 battalion. I can't remember if the latter was decided to be a good thing or not, but the demise of Support Company was certainly a retrograde move as far we were concerned. Tony Harrison, now married, remains a good and highly respected friend.

Emplaning from Libya after Ex Starlight.

After Support Company, I became the Assistant Adjutant to Iain Ferguson, the first time I was entrusted with staff work, admittedly of a very basic nature. I was also the Intelligence Officer and on exercise had to accompany Colonel George Burnett in the back of his open top Landrover sharing the very limited space with a signaller and George's very large Alsatian dog called Wylie. Not a very comfortable arrangement when we exercised across Salisbury Plain and I was supposed to be doing the map reading, especially when it was snowing hard. Early in 1960 the battalion deployed along with the rest of the brigade to North Africa on Exercise Starlight designed to test the UK strategic reserve in mounting and conducting operations overseas. We landed near Derna in Cyrenacia and fought our way along the Libyan coast rather as Generals Auchinleck, O'Connor and Rommel and later Montgomery had done in 1941 and 1942. It was exhilarating driving across miles of desert in open vehicles and engaging with an enemy force which we pushed back to the west as far as the exercise rules permitted. It was the first time I had been abroad for any length of time and the enjoyment I got from soldiering under as near realistic conditions as possible in peacetime, finally decided me to convert from a National Service to a regular commission and to make the Army my career. Clearly a decision that was to determine my future, my concern at the time was whether the regiment would accept me for a regular commission.

After the exercise we returned to Tidworth to be informed that the battalion would in 1961 go back to London and a further spell of public duties. This was news which prompted some of us to start thinking about possibly applying for an overseas secondment. At the time there were British officer led indigenous forces in some of those colonies where independence had still to be granted or where in some cases the local population was becoming increasingly restive at the delay in doing so. Aden, the Trucial States, the Oman, Brunei and earlier larger colonies like Kenya, British Guiana and some in West Africa were all countries where local regiments had been formed to handle local insurrections. Thomas Boyd-Carpenter, an exact contemporary, and I therefore formed up to Colonel Alan Cathcart at RHQ and asked to be allowed to second to the Sultan of Muscat's Armed Forces in Oman and, much to our surprise, were given permission to do so.

Life at Tidworth had been interesting and introduced me to forms of warfare which could only be learnt in a field formation, but it was time to go elsewhere and to experience an entirely different form of overseas soldiering, one which Iain Ferguson, himself a former seconded officer with the King's African Rifles, once dismissed rather glibly as 'bush whacking'. I have always enjoyed Salisbury Plain with its panoramic vistas, big skies, glorious sunsets and its historical associations with the Ancient Britons, an aspect which its use as a major military training area has helped to preserve, and I was sorry to leave not only the battalion but also Wiltshire. Notwithstanding I had made many good friends at all levels in my first tour in a Scots Guards battalion, friendships which in most cases would endure throughout my career as a soldier and indeed beyond.

A Blue Funnel ship anchored off Aden.

Oman

I flew to Aden just after Christmas 1960 to undertake a four-month Arabic language course run by the Army for those going to serve on the Arabian Peninsula with the Aden Protectorate Levies, the Trucial Oman Scouts or the Sultan of Muscat's Armed Forces. The language school was near the airport at Khormaksar in the shadow of the massive rock which towers over the port and lends its name to the pipe tune '*The Barren Rocks of Aden*' played every morning on the local radio to wake the colony from its slumbers. Well known as a coaling station on the route via Suez to the Far East there was always a fascinating array of ships anchored offshore. However, all was not peaceful and the Adenis were beginning to press for independence from Britain and, in some quarters, for the establishment of political links with the Yemen to the north. These first stirrings of dissension had still to develop in 1960, but under ten years later a fully blown insurrection caused immense problems for the British Government and led eventually to a handover of power under the most difficult of circumstances, with the British Army heavily committed in maintaining order in the protectorate.

Learning Arabic was not easy and I don't think any of the twenty or so officers on the course could claim any great expertise after four months. We were taught by an Army Education Officer and a jolly Lebanese teacher who did their best. It was very hot and a combination of the heat and our inability to grasp such a difficult language occasionally gave rise to pranks (which we thought funny) being played on our Lebanese instructor, such as loading the overhead fan with pieces of blackboard chalk and then switching it on at full speed so that he was met by a hail of chalk bullets! Great fun but unkind.

Socially, Aden was a bit of a desert but Thomas and I made some good friends. Ken Trevaskis, the Governor, who later had a son in the regiment, befriended us taking us up country into the northern jebel hills of the protectorate when he went to meet local tribal rulers. This was supposed to aid our learning of Arabic. David Trappes Lomax, from the Scots Guards was also on the Colony's military staff at the time, while I became friendly with Ken Irwin, a Superintendent in the Aden Police, and his wife Kathy who later asked me to be godfather to their son Aidan, born in 1961. Unfortunately, I lost touch with the Irwins when I left for the Oman, something which always perturbed me because of my vows to their baby son but, quite miraculously, Aidan and I were reunited in 2016 when his sister, Leslie Vaughan, spotted my name on a list of those attending the sixtieth anniversary of my leaving Eton in 1956, and sought me out. Her husband David was a contemporary.

In May 1961 I left Aden to fly to Muscat and a new military experience. I have often mused about why I decided to go to the Oman. Apart from a wish to avoid the straight jacket of further public duties, I had become fascinated by the Arab way of life – in particular that of the Bedouin tribesmen – who roamed the vast, arid desert wastes of the Empty Quarter or Rub al Khali of

Saudi Arabia, then one of the World's last unexplored wildernesses. Wilfred Thesiger's book *Arabian Sands* had made a deep impression on me and I decided I wanted to see the sands for myself. It was therefore fortuitous that the Army should give me the chance to go to the region. I might say that I was not the first Briton to be intrigued by the romanticism of the Arab tribes; countless others, including some famous explorers, had travelled the area between the Eastern Mediterranean and the Indian Ocean in search of the authentic Arab tribesmen long before I was to get there.

The history of the Sultanate of Oman as an independent state goes back to the seventeenth century when the country was an important and influential trading nation in the Middle East. Over subsequent centuries first the Portuguese and later the British came to influence the country, its rulers and its mercantile activities. In May 1961 when I arrived at Bait al Falaj, the Headquarters of the Sultan of Muscat's Armed Forces (SAF), the country was ruled by Sultan Said bin Taimur, an autocratic leader with little idea of the real world and no intention of modernising his own kingdom nor wish to improve the lot of his people. He lived in virtual isolation at Salalla in the extreme south and was always reputed to keep most of his personal wealth in a trunk under his bed!

Many books have been written about Oman which is now a prosperous state with all the attributes of a modern country. This remarkable change came about following a bloodless coup in 1970 when Sultan Said was overthrown and replaced by his son, Qaboos bin Said, whose benign leadership has led to vast improvements for his people with Oman recently being assessed by the United Nations as one of the world's most improved states. A combination of the discovery of oil and natural gas in large quantities and the wise investment of the resulting revenues in public infrastructure has been mainly responsible for this situation. Tourism is also a major national earner and many British people now visit the country.

However, in 1961, the position was very different. The Sultan had with British military assistance, only recently overcome an insurgency in the northern part of the country when a group of mountain tribesmen had attempted to overthrow his rule. They were backed by Egyptian money and propaganda and the insurrection could not have been defeated without the support of the British Army, in particular the SAS who mounted a series of daring raids onto the 10,000 feet high Jebel Akhdar (Green Mountain) plateau in 1959, after which the revolt collapsed. It was following these events that the Sultan's Army was expanded, modernised and greater numbers of contract and seconded British officers recruited to help to lead the force. The overall commander was Colonel Hugh Oldman and I was to be posted to C Company of the Northern Frontier Regiment (NFR) based on the Jebel Akhdar at a village called Saiq. I discovered my Company Commander was to be Major John Cooper, a contract officer recently retired from the SAS who had led one of the SAS squadrons assaulting the Jebel in 1959. Coincidentally he was a former Scots Guardsman who had fought with the Long Range Desert Group in North Africa in the early 1940s and had later been parachuted into occupied France to support the Resistance. A courageous and entertaining soldier with at least one Military Cross to prove it, we developed a great rapport.

John Cooper.

Arriving at Saiq in May 1961 struck me as what joining the French Foreign Legion must have been like. I had been dispatched on foot with a couple of soldiers to guide me, to climb the Jebel from Battalion Headquarters at Nizwa, to arrive 5,000 feet and six hours later at the top to be greeted by a gleaming white 'Beau Geste' fort and an ice-cold beer proffered by John Cooper! I was to be his second in command. C Company was an all Arab company drawn from most of the tribes in Oman whereas the other two rifle companies in the NFR were predominantly Baluchi; this reflected Sultan Said's obsession with not having too many ethnic Omanis in his Army lest their loyalty be put under too great a strain in times of difficulty. The Baluchis were recruited from Mekran in Baluchistan, just across the Persian Gulf on the opposite shore to Oman; there had long been close links between the two countries.

C Company was organised on British Army lines with three platoons commanded by Arab staff sergeants. They were called Darwish, Hamdan Sulieman and Saif Ali and were all likeable rogues! The key link to our Arab soldiers by John and me, the only two British personnel unless we had a visiting non-commissioned officer from one of the British battalions in Bahrain or Aden, was our locally commissioned officer, Lieutenant Said bin Salem. Said was a remarkable man: he had no education and originally applied to join SAF from Sohar where he was virtually homeless; he then worked his way up the ranks, taught himself to speak English but was never able to write it, and eventually rose to the highest level becoming ADC and eventually Chamberlain to Sultan Qaboos when he took over ruling Oman in 1970. John and I were fortunate to have such a man with us.

Said bin Salem.

Said has remained a good friend ever since those days and when he comes to the UK we sometimes meet at his house in Weybridge. In 2008 he invited Rosa and myself to stay with him in his family home in Muscat; it was an enjoyable visit and gave me the chance to show Rosa the areas where I had served fifty years before, although such have been the changes in the intervening period, that some places were by then unrecognisable. On that occasion I found the contrast with the 'old' Oman that I had known rather disconcerting and a little sad. They say one should never go back somewhere where you have had a wonderful experience since you will always be disappointed by what you find.

I might say that staying with Said in his own house in 2008 was quite challenging. Arab attitudes to women are different from those practised in the west and it was obvious from the start of our visit that Said was not really comfortable at being in the presence of female European visitors, especially when we had meals together. Such occasions required tact but were not easy although Said was always very dignified. As was to be expected, Rosa read the signs correctly and proved a model of careful behaviour. Fatima, Said's second wife, was however very sophisticated and Rosa and she hit it off well. None of this came as a great surprise since we knew there would be cultural difficulties in a country where the mixing of the sexes is frowned upon and can be inhibiting, but nonetheless we needed to be alert.

In 1961 our role on the Jebel was to provide a presence and to continue to root out certain dissident elements, still entrenched in the tribal areas where hitherto the Sultan's remit had not penetrated. Hours of patrolling and the laying of ambushes were undertaken and we had some successes although the opposition gradually faded away. Patrols, operations to interdict known terrorist routes and what were known as 'flag waving' marches mounted to impress the local people that we represented the Sultan's authority, were all part of military life. We marched for long periods over the mountains, calling on local tribal sheiks, spending hours partaking of coffee or a meal – usually hastily prepared dishes of goat meat, rice and dates – with those friendly to authority; it was exhausting work and often frustrating when conversation moved beyond the level of my rudimentary Arabic. Said was a good interpreter but how much he withheld from John and me I was never sure.

Muscat.

Jebel Misht.

Loading donkeys at the end of a patrol.

Our Arab soldiers were a cheerful lot and I was always grateful for the fact that I served in an Arab company and not a Baluchi one; the latter soldiers always appeared to me rather devious and sometimes disdainful of the local people. I never felt entirely comfortable with them. How reliable our Arabs would have been had we had to deal with a major confrontation involving protracted fighting, was hard to gauge; tribal loyalties were complex and John and I often felt a soldier's first loyalty might have been to his tribal elders rather than to the Sultan; in the event of battle being joined some might quietly have melted away. Luckily such a situation was never put to the test.

During my twenty months in Oman the company rotated around a number of places in the northern half of the country. In Ibri we were on the edge of the Empty Quarter and patrolled the fringes of the great desert having a camel troop to assist passage over the sands. In Saiq we had a donkey troop to help carry water and ammunition along the winding jebel paths while at Rostaq on the coastal side of the mountains, we used to patrol deep into the Jebel Akhdar up wadis the sides of which rose thousands of feet above us. It was awe inspiring country but extremely hard going and I became very fit. Our equipment was very basic and we patrolled wearing shorts and Bata desert boots which wore out very quickly on the rough going. Since overland transport was often impossible over poor or non-existent roads, we were regularly re-supplied by air. SAF had its own air force flown by seconded RAF pilots, which comprised some prop driven Provost attack aircraft for close support and a small number of Canadian Beaver aircraft for resupply. We became quite adept at clearing gravel strips to allow the latter to land in an emergency. The pilots were an excellent bunch and provided a lifeline to those based in remoter places. It was uncomplicated and satisfying soldiering and I relished the chance to experience it.

Beaver aircraft on an emergency airstrip.

I served two commanding officers in my time in the NFR: Colonel John Harrington and Colonel Dougie Dalglish. Dougie was a lovely man but fairly idle which of course suited those of us deployed far from Nizwa. During my twenty months I met a number of fine soldiers, men of experience and great common sense, people who had in their time helped to hold a disintegrating British Empire together after 1945 as an increasing number of colonies looked to a future, independent from Britain. John Clark, the battalion second in command and Malcolm Denison, the Force Intelligence Officer were both shrewd Arabists, men who spoke fluent Arabic and could handle the most bizarre of local situations with aplomb and good sense. Along with John Cooper they all became staunch friends and I missed them when I left. Others whom I got to know who, like me, were seconded were Bill Stanford, whom I must now have known for sixty years or more and John Friedberger, a Cavalry officer and my opposite number in A Company.

A metalsmith in the suk (market) in Hamra.

Towards the end of my time I seriously contemplated staying in the Oman and becoming a contract officer. This would have meant leaving the British Army and the Scots Guards and probably devoting my future – anyway in the medium term – to life in the Middle East. At one stage I even toyed with the idea of trying to serve with the Trans Jordan police, then under British command. RHQ somehow got wind of what was going through my mind and John Swinton, the Regimental

Adjutant, forestalled further such thoughts by writing to tell me that I had been selected at the end of my tour in Oman to go as Adjutant of the 2nd Battalion in Kenya and that he hoped I would put aside any further thoughts of leaving the regiment. The same letter told me that Thomas Boyd-Carpenter, who throughout my time with the NFR had served with the Muscat Regiment, had been selected to be the Adjutant of the 1st Battalion in Malaysia.

Notwithstanding, it was with a heavy heart that I said my farewells to scores of British and Arab friends and left Muscat to return to Britain just before Christmas 1962.

George Ramsay and Campbell Graham with the lion cubs.

Kenya

The 2nd Battalion Scots Guards had deployed to 24th Infantry Brigade in Kenya in early 1962. By the time I arrived a year later the battalion was based at Kahawa, a newly constructed military cantonment about ten miles north of Nairobi. Along with the other two battalions in the Brigade – the Gordon Highlanders and the Staffordshire Regiment – the Scots Guards were to be amongst the last British units to be based in Kenya. Ten years previously the colony had experienced an uprising by local tribes against British rule which led to a protracted and very violent campaign of civil disobedience against the Colonial power, resulting in many deaths amongst both the European settlers and the local people. It was in the aftermath of the Mau Mau rebellion, that, once order had been restored, Kenya, along with its close neighbours in East Africa – Tanganyika and Uganda – was to be granted independence from Britain in the latter half of 1963. The British Army was there to ensure the smooth transition of sovereignty.

Colonel George Ramsay was commanding the battalion and, after taking over from Anthony Hopkinson, I became his Adjutant. The RSM, Campbell Graham, was my right-hand man; a Scots Guardsman of great energy and forceful personality, he ruled firmly but with a degree of compassion and rough kindness. He was a great character and an outstanding guardsman, fiercely loyal to his regiment and to those with whom he served but was never lost for a word!

Kenya was a lovely country with a very pleasant climate, wonderful scenery and plenty of absorbing things to do if you enjoyed watching game, shooting, climbing, visiting the Indian Ocean beaches or simply ascertaining what was to be discovered by travelling around to see it all for yourself. Likewise, Uganda and Tanganyika had much to offer those prepared to travel. The region contained the two highest mountains in Africa – Kilimanjaro and Mt Kenya – and the almost as high Rwenzori range lay on Kenya's western border with Uganda. Colonial Kenya was a fast-moving society although when the battalion was there, probably less fast than had been the case in earlier years, the imminent prospect of the handover of government to the local African people meaning that the old order was beginning to fracture.

Mt Kenya.

The appointment of Malcolm MacDonald, the son of the first ever Labour Prime Minister, Ramsay MacDonald, to be the Governor in 1963 made clear the British Government's intention to transfer power at an early moment.

Zanzibar.

The battalion worked hard and played hard. Scope for training in both jungle and conventional warfare was considerable and all companies deployed to various corners of the region at some time. In addition, Left Flank went to Zanzibar, a small island off the coast of Tanganyika, for four months to provide a military presence there while, three months later, the whole battalion deployed to the two main islands of Zanzibar and Pemba to supervise the elections held in August 1963, prior to the grant of independence at the end of that year. However, the British Government's carefully crafted handover plans broke apart in January 1964 when the minority Arab government, elected a month previously, was overthrown by the African opposition in a coup following a very unpleasant bout of inter-communal violence. The battalion at Kahawa was put on alert to fly to the islands to restore the legitimate government but authority to deploy was never given; whether the British Government eventually came to realise the delicate situation that could have arisen had such action been taken so soon after the grant of independence, or whether Jomo Kenyatta, the Prime Minister of newly independent Kenya, baulked at assisting an operation by the former colonial power against a neighbouring state and therefore refused permission for British troops to be deployed from Kenyan soil, was unclear at the time. For the battalion it was a period of great frustration as we waited fully equipped to fly to Zanzibar, if necessary prepared to land against armed opposition, for orders which never came.

The previous month the battalion had participated in Kenya's own independence celebrations. Prince Philip represented the Queen at the formal handover ceremonies and the battalion provided a marching party and the Pipes and Drums to participate in the various ceremonies which took place in the newly built Uhuru (freedom) stadium in Nairobi. It was a period of great rejoicing and at the time the portents for a stable and well led independent Kenya appeared promising.

However, following the revolt in Zanzibar a series of mutinies amongst the residual armed forces of the by then independent East African countries broke out. These uprisings had their genesis principally in tribal rivalries fanned by a wish to exercise newly acquired political power, something exacerbated by the fact that the process of converting the former King's African Rifles battalions into local Army units, such as the Kenya and Uganda Rifles, had possibly taken place too quickly. The first revolt happened in January at Dar es Salaam in Tanganyika when 45 Commando Royal Marines had to be sent by sea from Aden to intervene to snuff out an uprising in the capital before it could spread across the rest of the country. Next the Ugandan Army staged a coup against its officers which was dealt with by the Staffords sent from Kenya and reinforced by Right Flank from the Scots Guards, commanded by Douglas Prior, the company being flown in to Entebbe Airport to deal with the mutineers at Jinja on the northern shores of Lake Victoria. On that occasion Jomo Kenyatta, doubtless realising that his own authority and that of his regional counterparts could also be under threat, readily agreed to the dispatch of British troops from Nairobi to support Prime Minister Milton Obote in Kampala.

Finally, problems arose in Kenya, both in Nakuru and later in Nairobi, when there were stirrings of dissent within the Kenyan Army. Those of us in Battalion Headquarters who had seen the domino effect of the mutinies in the other East African countries were not surprised. In Kenya action was taken to forestall further trouble by the deployment of Battalion HQ and a rifle company to Police Headquarters in Nairobi, a move which came as a great relief to Commissioner Catling and his senior officers. It was not long before the various uprisings across East Africa were brought under control and the democratically elected governments reasserted themselves everywhere, with British troops being able to return to barracks. One long term consequence of the uprisings was that Tanganyika and Zanzibar joined together to form one country – Tanzania – a logical move both geographically and politically. The manner in which the uprisings were handled – a combination of realistic diplomatic co-operation between nations and the deployment of military force to provide just the right level of intervention – was at the time hailed as a text book example of how such situations should be addressed and rightly so.

Murchison Falls on the White Nile, Uganda.

My job as Adjutant of the battalion was that of staff officer to the Commanding Officer, a task which required planning and disseminating the latter's orders. I was also in a sense his eyes and ears and had particular responsibility for disciplining the young officers. It was hard work entailing long hours, and sometimes brought me into conflict with the company commanders who were quick to react if they thought their own responsibilities were being threatened. Tony Boam in particular liked to have a go at Battalion HQ from time to time – no doubt sometimes for good reason – but luckily Roddy Ingham-Clark, his second in command, was usually able to tip me off by sending a coded telephone message warning me that the 'frosty wind was blowing in my direction'! However, I managed to make and maintain several friendships; Duncan Nicol and MIE Scott both of whom served as my assistants at various stages; John Gibb; Lorne Campbell; Peter Thomas who came out to Kenya with the Irish Guards in late 1963; Donald Whyte and Fred Adams the battalion's two Quartermasters and several others. The company commanders at the time were Douglas Prior, Tony Boam and 'Bwana' Scott with Tony Plummer and later Henry Blosse Lynch commanding No 3 Company Irish Guards, attached to us for a year in 1964.

During one of the periods the battalion was in barracks at Kahawa, RSM Campbell Graham acquired two lion cubs for the Sergeants' Mess. I think they were probably orphans. As might be expected they caused something of a sensation but suitable accommodation was found for them and they thrived. Some people suggested their eventually returning to Britain with the battalion, one particular flight of fancy even envisaging them being paraded when the battalion next mounted royal duties in London, a notion not smiled upon in official circles. In the end they were given to the cast of the film 'Born Free' which portrayed the work of George and Joy Adamson who had for years been returning lions taken into captivity, back into the wild. That move was successful although the lion eventually attacked and killed an African and had to be shot.

I have already made mention of the scope which East Africa and indeed adjacent areas of the continent offered for travel and discovery. Not all took advantage of the ease with which one could get around and officers and non-commissioned officers tended to be the most prolific travellers. Many guardsmen had little interest in wildlife although trips to the Kenya coast at Mombasa were always popular with everybody, but I suspect some of the less adventurous found life difficult at times. I was fortunate that Lorne Campbell, a couple of years older than me and commanding Headquarter Company in the battalion suggested early in 1964 we should drive to South Africa in his Humber Super Snipe, a large and heavy car which bounced across the corrugations on the mainly dirt roads which were the norm outside most African towns and cities. We planned a journey which would take us from Kenya, south across Tanganyika and through Northern and Southern Rhodesia to Salisbury, the capital of the latter colony. From there we visited the Victoria Falls and the recently built Kariba Dam before driving on to Beit Bridge where we crossed the Limpopo river into South Africa. Thereafter we travelled to Pretoria, Cape Town and along the 'garden route' to Durban.

It was a magnificent journey, a chance for us both to experience a part of the world we might never otherwise have seen. The country was breath taking and the people we encountered generally friendly, while the political events about which we learnt were fascinating. Events leading to change and disruption were about to unfold everywhere we went and subsequently did, with consequences foreseen by very few at the time, although Prime Minister

Harold MacMillan had anticipated some of the developments to come when he had made his prophetic 'winds of change' speech in Cape Town a few years earlier. At that time Southern Rhodesia presented a very attractive prospect: stable and possessed of rich agricultural land heavily populated by white settlers, many of whom had moved south from East Africa when change threatened there, but the first signs of a restive local population were apparent when we passed through Salisbury. Notwithstanding, to me a night in the Victoria Falls Hotel – rather reminiscent of the Adelphi Hotel, Liverpool in its design and decor – and the memorable experience of seeing the stupendous river Zambesi falls with the statue of David Livingstone positioned on the southern side at the spot at which he first sighted them, somehow seemed to say 'this is the way it will always be' but it was not to be and less than ten years later Southern Rhodesia had become Zimbabwe to face a grim future almost from the moment of independence.

Victoria Falls.

We found South Africa rather a menacing country. Ruled by an Afrikaans Government practising a policy of separate development or *apartheid*, the nation was clearly set on a collision course between its white population and its indigenous African peoples. Many of the nuances of the situation probably escaped Lorne and myself, but we saw and heard enough to tell us trouble was not far away and so it proved as the white dominated political system came to be increasingly threatened by violent demonstrators demanding change, leading eventually and inevitably to the conceding of power. After I left the Army thirty years later Rosa and I visited South Africa twice to stay with, amongst others, Philip and Fiona Erskine at the Cape and his cousin Anthony and his wife Diana in Natal, enjoying the beauty and opportunities offered in a land which seemed in 1964 to be blessed with so many advantages. However, it is necessary to record later developments, including the statesman-like way in which F.W. de Klerk and Nelson Mandela negotiated the transition which allowed South Africa to undertake regime change from white to African rule without undue bloodshed. Sadly, events since then have led to the virtual creation of a one party state in South Africa, as had already seemingly occurred in most African nations, leading to a marked decline in the country's economic and political circumstances.

At the end of our journey I flew back to Kenya and Lorne took a boat from Durban to Mombasa along with our faithful Humber car, and during his voyage met his future wife, Lizzie.

Another trip, again undertaken with Lorne, along with Roddy Ingham-Clark and Peter Thomas was to Marsabit in Kenya's Northern Frontier District, not far from Lake Rudolph, the largest permanent desert lake on the planet, 150 miles long and 20 miles wide now known as Lake Turkana. The NFD was a very arid, remote area in the northern part of the country which few people visited, either because of its inaccessibility or because entry was officially restricted since it was increasingly being infiltrated by Somali shifta gangs marauding across the border from the north. At the time that didn't bother us and we spent a happy few days camped at a guest house beside a watering hole in a jungle clearing where elephants and other wild life came at night. To us it represented the essence of life in Africa in 1964: sitting out under the stars on a warm night, cold beer in hand, watching game, yarning to each other and experiencing what seemed to us to epitomise life in the bush.

Kilimanjaro.

Some of the party who climbed Kilimanjaro wih our guides.

During 1964, I climbed both Mt Kenya and Kilimanjaro, taking with me a group of guardsmen on each occasion; others did the same and indeed my future wife, Rosa, climbed Kilimanjaro too although before she met me. She had gone out to Nairobi to help David and Flippy MacDonald-Milner with their children a few months before the battalion returned to Britain at the end of 1964. David was a Welsh Guardsman and at the time on the military staff in Nairobi. Rosa knew Flippy's family from Gloucestershire and David and Flippy remain good friends to this day. Such contacts as these and others during my time in Kenya led to some wonderful friendships, in the case of Rosa turning out to be a very special one indeed! Included in my other contacts made in Kenya were several white settlers like Derek and Pat Fisher living near Nanyuki and Fabian Wallis at Thompson's Falls, all sadly now dead.

Four months before the battalion left Kenya to return to Britain, George Ramsay handed over command to Michael Gow. George's tenure had been a very busy one with plenty of military activity to keep the battalion on its toes; he handled the situations which arose with aplomb while at the same time keeping a close eye on how his guardsmen conducted themselves when under the spotlight of Kenyan public opinion. Scope for poor publicity was always present and it was greatly to the credit of all ranks from George downwards that there were few embarrassing moments to spoil an otherwise fine reputation. As his Adjutant I should know!

My friendship with George lasted until his death in 2016 and it gave me enormous pleasure when his son Alec became my Adjutant in 1977 when I was commanding the 2nd Battalion in Germany. Meanwhile Michael Gow became a good friend too, his short time in Kenya seeing a round of parades and parties to bring the battalion's three-year tour there to an end. We left Kahawa in November to return to Caterham Barracks in Surrey, the site of the former Guards Depot, to begin a tour of public duties. I was to remain as Adjutant until July 1965 and had quickly to learn the skills needed to manage the manpower and ceremonial factors inherent in providing soldiers for Royal duties from a barracks, twenty miles outside Central London.

Marriage

The contrast between Kenya and Caterham will be obvious to all and, once the battalion had settled back in Britain, it got on with the task of finding soldiers to allow it to discharge its new and very different responsibilities. The role was repetitive and unexciting and the scope for error considerable. One early unforeseen event concentrated our thoughts when in late January 1965 Sir Winston Churchill, wartime Prime Minister and elder statesman, died. He was to be buried at Bladon in Oxfordshire a few weeks later following a state funeral in Central London. As Adjutant I had to prepare the battalion for a major part in the ceremonial proceedings when the coffin was taken from Westminster Hall where it had been lying in state, through the streets on a gun carriage to St Paul's Cathedral where, following the state funeral service, it was carried to Tower Pier, embarked on a Port of London Authority launch and taken upriver to Festival Pier, prior to being placed aboard a special train at Waterloo Station to be conveyed to Bladon.

Including the provision of street liners and a marching party, commanded by 'Bwana' Scott, the battalion had to find a total of almost five hundred men for duty that day leaving hardly a soldier in barracks. Michael Gow was in command at Tower Pier and, as his adjutant, I accompanied him there once we had seen the rest of the battalion deployed to their duties. Standing above the Thames watching the launch pull away from the pier was very poignant, particularly when the large quayside cranes lining the opposite bank lowered their jibs in a final, unrehearsed tribute to Sir Winston, as sixteen RAF Lightning aircraft flew overhead. It was a cold and overcast February day and the weather, the guardsmen in their Atholl Grey greatcoats and bearskins, the funeral marches played by the bands and the silence of the watching crowds, all added to the solemnity of the occasion. It was an enormous privilege to be involved.

In my last few months in Kenya I had met Rosemary Hicks Beach, the younger daughter of Bill and Diana Hicks Beach who lived at Witcombe near Gloucester; she was then staying in Kenya with David and Flippy MacDonald-Milner. For Rosemary or Rosa as she was always known by her family, her stay in Kenya was an opportunity to see something of the world outside Britain after her years as a pupil, either at Seven Springs near Cheltenham or later

Our wedding at Gloucester. 31st July 1965.

when boarding at Lawnside in the Malvern Hills. Fortunately or not for her, but certainly fortunate for me, we had met in Kenya and got together again when she returned home in early 1965.

We became engaged in February after I had asked Rosa's father for her hand. Bill, a prominent London solicitor with Payne, Hicks Beach in Lincoln's Inn, had been MP for Cheltenham for fourteen years retiring from Parliament in 1964. He and Rosa's mother, Diana, immediately welcomed me into the family as did her brother Mark and her elder sister, Liz. Our engagement was the start of a long and happy union of which in 2015 we celebrated fifty years. All marriages must be different; some work, some don't and end in discord and separation while most only survive through compromise and generosity of spirit. We were lucky that, despite all the minor upsets which must afflict everybody, we have managed to steer a pretty straight course through our married life together and have had the added joy of bringing up three most rewarding sons: Nicholas born in 1967, Hughie in 1968 and William in 1972. But that is leaping ahead and I still had work to do as the adjutant of my battalion, one being to ride alongside Michael Gow when he commanded the Mall street liners on the occasion of the 1965 Queen's Birthday Parade. It was the only time I was called upon to ride on a ceremonial parade and, in view of my natural disinclination for horses and riding, it was neither a very relaxed nor a very polished performance. At one moment Michael and I had to ask a mounted officer of the Metropolitan Police to give us a lead, since our horses obviously wanted to go home to Knightsbridge Barracks rather than heading up the Mall towards Horse Guards as we wished!

Riding in the Mall with Michael Gow on the Birthday parade 1965.

Presentation of new colours in Edinburgh 1965. DMN nearest on the left.

In July, the battalion moved temporarily to Edinburgh where The Queen was to present it with new colours. The parade was held in the gardens of the Palace of Holyroodhouse and was preceded or followed by a round of parties, including an officers' ball at the Assembly Rooms in George Street to which my parents, Diana Hicks Beach and Rosa all came. It was a marvellous few days. Thereafter, the battalion dispersed across Scotland to train or show the flag before concentrating near Oban for an exercise in which a notorious rebel fighter and his cohorts were to be hunted down and captured. The rebel leader was one, Hamish McPuke – alias Murray Naylor – and the exercise took place on the island of Mull in glorious summer weather, culminating in a sea battle between two Royal Naval auxiliary vessels, each armed with powerful sea hoses firing fish heads, carrying the battalion and the enemy contingent across the Firth of Lorn as the two sides returned to Oban. Commanding the enemy force was my last act as Adjutant before handing over my responsibilities to Mark Maxwell-Hyslop. I had had a wonderful two and a half years serving two excellent commanding officers – George Ramsay and Michael Gow – working with a multitude of people of different ranks, many of whom became firm friends. The closeness of military life, the trust and respect it engenders and the sheer thrill of being young and active in a wonderful country like Kenya, coupled with a varied and exciting military programme, meant that all of us in the battalion had had a most rewarding time. Fellow officers such as Peter Leng, Tony Harrison, 'Bwana' Scott, Tony Boam, Lorne Campbell, Henry Blosse Lynch and Peter Thomas, both of the Irish Guards, MIE Scott, Duncan Nicol and Roddy Ingham-Clark, the latter two now sadly dead, and RSM Campbell Graham and other senior ranks all became staunch friends and most remain so to this day.

My wedding to Rosa took place on 31st July when we were married in Gloucester Cathedral by the Dean, the Very Rev Seriol Evans. As might be imagined it was a wonderful day: glorious weather – Summer 1965 really smiled upon us – a church full of guests, a lovely reception at Witcombe generously given by my new in laws, and great happiness all round; we were indeed a lucky couple. Bill gave Rosa away and brother Christopher was my best man. Colonel Roddy Hill, a highly respected wartime Coldstreamer and Rosa's uncle proposed our health, briefly saying "In my day I came down to Witcombe to marry a Hicks Beach and now Murray has sensibly done the same thing". Afterwards we spent our first night as a married couple at the

Compleat Angler Hotel, Marlow and then went on to spend our honeymoon in the Lebanon and Kenya, visiting several contacts from the battalion's time there. It was a wonderful three weeks.

Offiwers' tug of war team. (R to L): Tony Harrison; John Gibb; Philip Erskine (standing); Douglas Prior, Ian Mackay; Michael Gow and DMN.

Witcombe had been in the ownership of the Hicks Beach family for several generations. Located at the foot of the Cotswold Escarpment a mile below the village of Birdlip and equidistant from Gloucester and Cheltenham, the estate comprised a mixture of woodlands and arable land. There were also several coverts which provided for a pheasant shoot run by Bill and later improved to a very high standard by my brother in law, Mark. Don Hannis was the keeper for most of the time I shot there and his contribution was considerable. Some others who were members of the syndicate were Allan Hughes, a partner in Payne Hicks Beach, Ian Frazer, 'Bwana' Scott and, for a short time, Christopher Clayton.

Rosa's family were keen followers of the Cotswold Hunt and Diana, Liz and Rosa often rode to hounds. It was never a pastime which attracted me but the culture underlying hunting in rural areas of Britain was very strong and helped to maintain practices which, if abandoned, could have likely led to a diminishment of the rural ethos and possibly to unacceptable changes in the manner in which we keep our countryside looking the way it does, and has done for centuries. This is not the place to debate the rights and wrongs of hunting in rural Britain and recent years have anyway seen the adoption of a new approach, which allows the sport to continue albeit it in a more controlled way, a change now accepted by many but no means by all. For her part Rosa has always accepted the need for practical regulation and the requirement for hunting people to behave in a sensible, unprovocative manner, something which sadly a few still seem unable to understand. She herself is still hunting with the Middleton hounds in North Yorkshire which, if she first started at the age of eight, I calculate means she has been hunting for between sixty and seventy years. She was an extremely effective secretary of the Middleton Hunt for a number of years after we went to live in the Malton area in 1989.

I think I got on well with all my in laws. Bill sadly suffered a stroke before I could really get to know him and died in 1975 aged sixty-eight. Diana lived for nearly another forty years before dying peacefully at a residential home near York in 2002 where, to be close to Rosa, she had spent the last year of her life. Tragically Rosa's brother Mark died in 1998 at the age of fifty-nine leaving a widow and three children. One of his sons, Freddie Hicks Beach, is now the owner of Witcombe.

Rosa's elder sister, Liz Hinson, married twice; first to Simon Clarke and secondly to Peter Hinson. Her elder son Martin Clarke died of leukaemia in 2002 while working in America; Timmy, her second son is married with two sons and lives in Cambridge where he teaches drama at St John's College Prep School. Liz spent most of her life in East Sussex moving a few years ago to Mayfield where she was very happy, surrounded by a wide circle of friends who enjoyed similar interests; very sadly she died in March 2018 after suffering bone cancer in her last few months. Rosa has therefore lost her mother, two siblings and a nephew over the last twenty years, more than should reasonably be asked of anyone.

Our Ushers. (L to R): Simon Clark, Francis Baxendale, Thomas Boyd-Carpenter, David Gardiner, MIE Scott, Ian Pemberton, Mark Hicks Beach, Christopher Clayton, Colin Senior and Roddy Ingham Clark.

Our respective parents.

After our honeymoon and a spell staying with both her parents and mine, Rosa and I embarked on our married life together. Thereafter our travels were to take us to Germany where I was to work as a junior staff officer in Headquarters 4th Guards Brigade in the Westphalian town of Iserlohn. It was to be the first of four tours I was to undertake in the British Army of the Rhine (BAOR) between then and 1983. Since there was no accommodation for a recently married man as junior as I was, I had initially to go to Germany unaccompanied until my name came to the top of the Garrison housing list, when Rosa was able to join me. In fact, due to the kindness of Fane and Fiona Gaffney – Fane was a Welsh Guardsman also serving in the same Headquarters – we managed to borrow their house for a few weeks while they were back in England, prior to getting our own.

Germany

Over the next twenty years I was to serve or exercise in Germany on several occasions. British forces had been stationed in the northern half of the country ever since the end of the war in 1945, initially to oversee the peace, including the eventual re-building of the German nation, and later as part of the NATO alliance constructed to counter any potential Soviet threat to Western Europe. BAOR was the command which managed the peacetime deployment of British troops, of which at their height there were nearly 65,000 soldiers and airmen on German soil, while NORTHAG or to give it its full title the Northern Army Group, was the operational formation which would have commanded all British units in time of tension or war. Had it ever become necessary to deploy them, British ground forces would have occupied an area south of Hanover and north of Kassel close to the Inner Germany Border between Communist East Germany and democratic West Germany. Our raison d'etre for being in Germany was, by 1965, purely to assist in deterring any Soviet attack on Western Europe, a threat later greatly diminished after the fall of the Berlin Wall in 1989.

These therefore were the reasons why I served in Germany on so many occasions. BAOR was akin to working in a large corporation. In order to serve the needs of its servicemen and their families a comprehensive network of utilities had been developed over a number of years and these either supplemented or were superimposed upon the local German administrative structures. We lived amongst local communities but were not really integrated; while relations were mostly friendly, barriers of language and culture and no doubt feelings about the war which lingered in some minds for many years, inevitably meant that both sides tended to keep their distance. That said there were shared occasions and most British personnel enjoyed their time serving in Germany, an efficiently run nation with some lovely towns and countryside to be seen and enjoyed while, below the surface, there may have been more mutual interests than either nation might at the time have wished to acknowledge.

Iserlohn was a pretty town located a few miles south of the Ruhrgebeit, that industrial region which stretches across Westphalia and contains much of Germany's manufacturing capacity. Cities such as Essen, Dortmund and Dusseldorf with their concentration of heavy industries dominated the area.

My life as a very junior and inexperienced Grade 3 staff officer in the HQ was to assist in running the Brigade's operations and training. It was a very pleasant place to work and I enjoyed the company of Henry Hugh Smith, a captain in the Blues and Royals, who worked in the same office as me; he and I used to spend a lot of time rather childishly annoying people by connecting the most unlikely of callers to each other by manipulating the fiendishly efficient German military telephone network. We could then listen to the affronted reactions when people discovered they were being set up; it gave us a lot of fun! Others in the HQ included Brigadier Vernon Erskine Crum, John Acland and Tony Boam, all Scots Guardsmen. John Acland was later replaced as Brigade Major by Denis Lewey, a Coldstreamer, with whom I got on very well, rather better than with John. The latter was in my opinion a perplexing person; extremely able and invariably revered by those whom he commanded, he was very much a soldier's soldier. Sadly, his relationships with those senior to him were often less harmonious, particularly when he chose to be unkind or subversive. A great waste since he could well have had a glittering career, reaching the top of the Army. Meanwhile Denis died a few years later far too young, a great loss to the Army and his regiment. He and his wife Anne were really firm friends.

Our first married quarter was at 8. Rubenstrasse, a captain's quarter on what was generally known as 'the patch'. It was quite adequate for a couple living on their own although the arrival of Nicholas in March 1967 filled up most of the spare space. Nicholas was born in the British Military Hospital in Iserlohn (altogether there were four such hospitals in BAOR to cater for British Army and Air Force personnel) and for all that we were living in a foreign country, the whole process of childbirth might just as well have taken place in Britain.

Meg, our first dog, in Iserlohn.

The social life amongst those serving in Germany was always quite lively. We met a lot of fellow married couples of a similar age and there were plenty of regimental events. As a result, we got to know a wide range of people and when the opportunity arose, travelled around many parts of Europe. Prior to going to Iserlohn neither of us had really seen much of the Continent and so we made good use of being based in a place, which by virtue of the German autobahn network, allowed us to reach destinations not so accessible from Britain. Cheap flights and package tours were only just beginning to feature as a means of holidaying on the Continent, while some currency restrictions were still in place.

I always felt that living in BAOR was probably not unlike India between the wars. Germany was not our country, the culture was different, we would one day return home having completed the job we were sent to do and, while the necessity for our being there was generally understood, it was not always welcomed by the German population unless they lived close to the Inner German Border and harboured fears of what a Soviet invasion of the West might mean. That said, from a professional viewpoint, service in Germany provided a challenge and soldiering could be stimulating. It was however sometimes less satisfactory for some of the families who could often find time hanging heavily.

At the end of 1968 I was posted from Germany to return to join the 1st Battalion of the regiment in Edinburgh. I was to command Right Flank, taking over from Duncan Nicol with whom I had previously served in Kenya when he was my Assistant Adjutant. The battalion was commanded by Colonel Gregor McGregor and was based at Redford Barracks on the southern outskirts of the city. It had just returned from a tour in the Far East when it had been located at Terendak in Malaysia from where it had undertaken tours of duty in Sarawak and Sabah during low intensity defensive operations against Indonesia, in what at the time was known as 'Confrontation'.

Command of a company is always fun and I thoroughly enjoyed Right Flank where I was well supported by Andrew Parsons, the second in command and David Torrance and 'Dusty' Millar, respectively the CSM and CQMS. David Torrance was a first-class Warrant Officer while Dusty and I had worked together previously at platoon level. It made for a happy team. August that year saw part of the battalion deploy to Jamaica for jungle training and the battalion's two flank companies were included. We were based at Port Antonio in the North East corner of the island and platoons in Right Flank were commanded by Mark Tennant, Martin Snow and Jeremy Cox, the latter joining for the exercise. Jeremy had recently joined the regiment from the Cameronians, a Lowland Scottish infantry regiment which had earlier disbanded as part of a reduction in numbers of regiments. Robin Buchanan-Dunlop came to join us at the same time for the same reason; both Jeremy and he settled in quickly and both proved real assets to the Scots Guards.

The exercise was fun but not very strenuous, although Gregor and I had a slight altercation at one moment over the conduct of the training at the end of which he said 'The trouble with you, Murray, is that you are too like me'. I have never worked out if that was meant as a compliment or an insult. Later Kim Ross and I climbed the Blue Mountain, the highest point on the island and afterwards flew to Florida for a long week end where we stayed near Sarasota with a relation of his called 'Tishy' Groves, a retired RAF Group Captain, and his wife. It was my first experience of meeting Americans in their own country and the Sunshine State and the people we met there provided quite an insight; they seemed to be mainly retired, very conservative in their attitudes, prone to drinking rum cocktails for much of the day and spending a lot of their time lounging by a pool or on board a cabin cruiser fishing in the Gulf of Mexico! We had a great two days and, as always with Americans, we were royally looked after and, wherever we went, were met with genuine friendship. Kim was a delightful companion, one of the warmest and most considerate officers to serve in the regiment in my time.

In Florida with Kim Ross and his relative, 'Tishy' Groves.

In Edinburgh, Rosa and I lived in a married quarter close to Redford Barracks. While we were there Hughie was born in the Simpson Memorial Pavilion, an annex to the Infirmary. I have never been one to wish to be involved when his wife gives birth – a practice which now seems universal – and I was later told that when Rosa was about to go into labour the gynaecologist tried to call me to summon me to the hospital. At the same time, I was on the telephone to him to discover how Rosa was doing so our calls cancelled each other out, much to my relief!

In 1969, the battalion left Edinburgh and moved to Chelsea Barracks in London to undertake public duties. At the same time Gregor McGregor handed over command to Colonel Murray de Klee, an experienced operational soldier who had commanded G Squadron of the SAS. I got on well with Murray, liked and respected him for his no nonsense and effective approach to command of a battalion deployed in London to undertake public duties and found him easy to serve. Indeed, the battalion had a very busy summer of public duties culminating in trooping its Queen's Colour on the Birthday Parade in June. Murray commanded the parade and Alec Ramsay, George's son, carried the Queen's Colour. I had the honour of commanding the Escort to the Colour and managed to do my bit without any awful mistakes. It was the first of three occasions when I commanded a guard on the Queen's Birthday Parade, the others being in 1973 and 1974.

Escort to the Colour 1969. DMN, Alec Ramsay and Martin Snow.

In London, Rosa and I lived in a married quarter in Putney. 1 Coldstream Gardens had not long been built and it and the other quarters just off West Hill Road were intended for those serving in Central London. It was a forty-minute commute by the District Line to Sloane Square and being on the A3 road meant we could get out of the metropolis fairly easily. The house itself was a little strange, being open plan and rather like a studio, but it was comfortable enough and we enjoyed our year there. I recollect lying in bed and watching Neil Armstrong landing on the Moon in 1969.

While still in Edinburgh I had sat the Army's Staff College Exam to assess whether or not I might be a suitable candidate to undergo staff training at Camberley. The exam was a bit of a marathon and consisted of eight mini-exams covering military strategy, tactics, current affairs, assistance to the civil power, military law and the application of science to warfare amongst other subjects, lasting in all for two and a half days when we sat in the Redford Barracks gymnasium, writing feverishly. Before the first paper we had to fill in a form asking us to say where we would like to go, assuming we were successful in the exam which was, of course, a big 'if'. The options were the British Army staff college at Camberley, either of the other two service colleges at Greenwich or Bracknell, or one of the 'old' Commonwealth colleges. I remember thinking that I ought to show loyalty to the Army and so wrote down Camberley first, followed by the RN college at Greenwich, followed by India. I then waited.

Eventually I heard that I had passed and a little time later Tony Harrison, the Scots Guards Regimental Adjutant, accosted me from behind a pillar in the Guards Chapel where Rosa and I were attending a wedding, and said "Psst... it's India." I had been selected to go to the Defence Services Staff College at Wellington in South India on a year long course beginning in January 1970. Once we had got over our initial surprise, Rosa and I had to start thinking about what we would need to take which meant contacting Dennis Williams, a Gunner attending the 1969 course whom I was to replace, and then making a list of the sort of necessities taken for granted in Britain but probably unobtainable in India. The NAAFI HQ in Kennington, in the shape of a Mr Chitty, was extremely helpful and between us we put together a package of seemingly vital commodities, although we wouldn't know if we had made the right choices until we reached Wellington.

Before I left the battalion, the latter deployed on an exercise to Northern Germany and Denmark. It was a way of getting everybody out of London in order to provide a complete break from public duties. We sailed across the North Sea, disembarked at Wilhelmshaven and then moved to Neustadt near Kiel where we embarked in German Marine landing craft as a prelude to making a seaborne assault on the Danish islands of Mon and Falster. The exercise was designed to test the NATO land rapid reaction force or the AMF(L) as it was known, and during the ten days we were on Danish soil we covered many miles and dealt with a number of hostile situations – including genuine peace protesters who were certainly not peaceful – before returning home. It was a thoroughly enjoyable exercise and a tonic for the battalion after a heavy stint of London ceremonial.

India.

January 1970 saw Rosa, the two boys and me emplaning at RAF Brize Norton to fly to Bahrain on the first leg of our journey to Wellington in South India. From there we transferred to a BOAC flight to Bombay where we landed at 4am to find the transit lounge at the airport a vast dormitory with hundreds of Indians dossed down to sleep! We soon learnt that this was a normal feature of life on the sub-continent where any public place such as an airport, a railway station or a city street were fair game for a night's kip!

Our onward journey to Wellington was further disrupted because Bangalore Airport was fog bound and so we had to fly to Madras before later going on to Bangalore. I recall sitting in the airport at Madras that first morning wondering what we might safely have for breakfast; so unsure were we of where we were and what we might eat which would not immediately give us upset tummies that, I think, we hardly ate a thing! We had travelled thus far with James and Alison Hamilton Russell and their three children since they too were bound for Wellington where James was also to attend the staff course. James was in the Blues and Royals and like me a major. From Bangalore we eventually climbed aboard three taxis – one for each family and a third for the luggage – and then drove the two hundred or so miles to the staff college over the Western Ghats or coastal range of hills to reach Wellington, a small township in Madras State or as it is now known Tamil Nadu, approximately four hundred miles north of Cape Comorin, the southernmost point of India, and the same distance south west of Madras, the state capital. The name of the latter has also now been altered to Chennai.

The journey had been tiring, hot, fraught with the first experiences of Indian bureaucracy and doubts that we had made the right decision to opt for Wellington but all that was to change. We eventually arrived around 6pm at the Wellington Gymkhana Club set amongst beautiful tea gardens and stands of eucalyptus trees where we were to stay for our first few days, but the greatest boost to morale came when we met Gracie, our Indian ayah, a wonderfully poised and reassuring woman to whom all four of us immediately took. She remained with us the whole year until we returned to England in November and added enormously to the enjoyment of our time in Wellington.

Gracie.

Our first few days were taken up with finding our way around, making the usual contacts with the bank – cashing a cheque was always a time-consuming process involving at least half a dozen people and several ledgers – finding a doctor, hiring a car, discovering the shops, moving into a married quarter and meeting some of our fellow students. There were four 'Brits' on the course; already mentioned was James Hamilton Russell, from the Royal Navy Tony Wilks, a recently divorced Lieutenant Commander and therefore single, while Squadron Leader Robert Wood, a fast jet pilot represented the RAF and was accompanied by his wife Amy and three children. We were a harmonious team and I think represented the UK quite well, an obligation made very clear to us by one or two ex-pats living in the area who had been scandalised by the behaviour of one of our predecessors on an earlier course!

Our quarter was 8/2 Wellington Hall, a semi-detached building set in a row of identical houses; our neighbours were an Indian naval officer and his wife and many other students lived around about. The house was basic: two bedrooms upstairs, an open plan ground floor which included a study so that I could do my course work in comparative peace, running water but no bath, a substitute for which was a tin tub which would be filled up by Muthu, our bearer, who every evening would carry some old paraffin flimsies filled with hot water upstairs, finally announcing "Bathwater ready, sahib" when the task was completed – a time honoured ritual! Muthu's wife Fatima was our cook and we also had the services of Camalo who was officially a sweeper but undertook various other less complicated tasks. Along with Gracie they were a team who had looked after many previous British students and we were lucky to have them, although Muthu in particular tried our patience at times. I have already said the house was basic, the kitchen particularly so, and if you shone a torch there at night the sight of the cockroaches would have concerned you!

The 'real India'. The last of seven temples at Mahalipuram on the Bay of Bengal. The other six have been submerged by the sea.

An early decision to be made was a car. India in the 1970s produced three European cars under licence: a Morris Oxford called the Ambassador, a Fiat and a Triumph Herald. We opted for the last and hired one from Doctor Munu, a local dentist whose side line was renting out cars. It was always contended that he did better with his cars than with people's teeth and that, if a hirer had a problem with their vehicle, the good doctor would leave a dental patient in mid consultation to see to the needs of the car. Our Herald did us well and we travelled quite extensively across South India, something which I believe those British families who go to Wellington now are advised not to do because of the risks posed by increasing traffic and lawless locals, a development to be regretted since there is less chance of seeing the 'real' India.

Another local character, who could possibly be described as a 'relic' from the days of the Raj, was Mrs Pearson Powis who lived locally and was conveyed everywhere in a chauffeur driven battered Austin A40, and whom we used to meet at the local Anglican Church most Sundays. She was always alleged to have murdered her husband but gave all the appearances of being a charming, rather sweet old lady; one Sunday in September just before Tony Wilks and I were to depart on the College land tour, Tony told her we would be away for a few weeks and would not see her until our return, to which she replied, "I shall be here, but I am not sure about you"!

Wellington had long been a military cantonment and in 1970 was the home of the Madras Regiment as well as the Indian Defence Services Staff College. India's staff college pre-partition had been at Quetta which in 1947 became part of Pakistan. The town of Wellington was really no more than a village, sandwiched between Coonor and the much bigger town of Ootacamund or 'Ooty' or 'Snotty Ooty' as it was known in the days of the Raj. Pre-independence it was the place to which the state government in Madras would migrate to escape the hot weather on the shores of the Bay of Bengal. It contained the Ooty Club and a racecourse where the Staff College held a race day in which Rosa rode and, if I remember, beat the Commandant (or was it at the point to point meeting held on the Downs above Wellington?); in any case beating the Commandant was something no Indian student or their wives would have dared to do! The country surrounding Wellington was lovely: tea gardens and gum trees and at 5,000 feet beautifully cool with refreshing breezes, only interrupted in September by the north-east monsoon. A steam powered narrow gauge rack railway connected the plateau comprising the Nilgiri hills with the plains below at the railhead station of Mettupalayam from where it was possible to travel to Madras and other destinations. There was also a torturous winding road down to Mettupalayam and both routes took several hours to negotiate.

My sponsor on the staff course was a lieutenant colonel called Som Somana, an Indian Guards officer and therefore a logical choice to look after a fellow guardsman; both he and his wife Reynu were charming and very kind and considerate to Rosa and myself. He rose to high rank but is sadly no longer alive. The calibre of officers on the course, both instructors and students, was pretty high. In addition to the four Brits there were some other foreigners: an American major and a naval officer – Fran Juno and his wife Diane, and the Stevens – with a Canadian called Mel and his wife Em, and representing Australia, 'Col' and Cyn Bryant, the latter four, as might have been expected, all fairly brash. Then there were a Frenchman, Bernard Forrer, who didn't speak much English, a charming Abyssinian called Afeworki and some rather doubtful chaps from Indonesia, Iraq and Syria. However, we all got along quite well and were known collectively as the 'officers from the friendly overseas countries'.

There were approximately 180 officers on the course, sixty of whom were from the Indian Navy or Air Force and the rest from the Army. Individual service structures were unsurprisingly very similar to those of the three British services, as was the approach to staff training and the teaching of tactics and strategy. Before I went to India some contemporaries had suggested that a year in India rather than at Camberley, might be a career disadvantage, principally because I would not have the opportunity to learn British staff work or get to know and develop friendships with people of my own age. In the event I don't think it mattered one iota and nine years later when I went as an instructor at the British Army Staff College at Camberley, it confirmed to me that the point was fallacious, even if well meant.

The routine at the college at Wellington was predictable: six terms in each of which we covered a different aspect of warfare. One term it was our ability to perfect the operational presentation of orders and messages and the use of military nomenclature known as 'staff duties'; another we studied internal security and how to operate with the civil authorities at times of internal unrest; we also studied 'plains' warfare when we analysed how the Indian Army might operate under semi-desert conditions against an adversary such as Pakistan while, at the other end of the spectrum we considered operations at high altitude in the Himalayas. The Indians had not forgotten that eight years previously they had been overrun by attacks in two areas along their Himalayan border with China – at the time the disputed McMahon line – which, had the Chinese pressed harder, could have penetrated deep into Northern India. I developed a great interest in this particular subject and, having whetted my appetite by reading a fascinating account in a book entitled '*India's China War*', was given a special task of writing a paper for the college listing the most relevant lessons to be learnt from the cross-border confrontations in 1962. It came to be known as the China Study and attracted a certain degree of ribaldry from some colleagues, especially Tony Wilks, but I think he was only jealous because the Naval wing never gave him a similar opportunity to show off his superior knowledge of naval affairs!

British officers with the UK High Commissioner and senior officers of the staff college with wives.

In parallel the college engaged several high-level speakers to come and talk to us once we turned our attention to the strategic, political and economic issues confronting the nation. President Giri, at the time India's president came, as did the Service Chiefs and many other notable people - industrialists, civil servants and others - including the UK High Commissioner, Sir Morrice James when he invested Tony with an MBE for his prior service captaining an RN patrol vessel on fishery protection patrols. More importantly Sir Morrice brought us a much-appreciated re-supply of Scotch whisky, as opposed to the Indian variety known as Red Knight which was apt to bring on a headache if consumed too quickly or too often!

It was an interesting year which involved external visits to various civil and military establishments, including three weeks living under canvas on the plains to the south of the Nilgiris when we were set practical staff problems to solve. On that occasion I shared a tent with three Sikh officers whose early morning preparations included combing their hair and beards, fitting their turbans, bangles and other accoutrements as required by their religion; such antics at an early hour further destroyed my sleep already made difficult by the very high temperatures.

In September the whole college travelled by train the length of India visiting a range of military stations to see the Indian armed services in their various bases. Bangalore, the centre of the nation's growing high-tech industries, Agra, Delhi, Deolali and Jhansi, the latter where we met the Indian armoured corps and some of us had the privilege of being invited to dine with the officers of Hodson's Horse, one of the oldest cavalry regiments in India, formed long before partition and still following customs and a culture originating from the days of Empire, were all on our itinerary. Possibly the most interesting day was at Bombay when we went to sea with the Navy and Tony Wilks and I were embarked on the cruiser INS *Delhi*. She had been built in Glasgow between the wars and as HMS *Achilles*, by then with the New Zealand Navy, had taken part with HMS *Exeter* and HMS *Ajax* in the Battle of the River Plate in 1939, when the three Royal Naval cruisers so disabled the German battleship *Graf Spee* as to cause her to be scuttled off Montevideo. After the war *Achilles* was sold to India and when we sailed in her in 1970 she was clearly nearing her end. As Tony said, "The old lady was wheezing steam from every pore" as we went out into the Indian Ocean.

That last expedition had a sequel since, when following disembarkation, Tony and I were walking back along the dockside, he espied a Russian built submarine tied up and flying the Indian flag. Conscious that he – and indeed also Robert Wood – had been encouraged by their respective services to discover anything of interest about foreign ships or aircraft purchased by the Indians and to pass it back to London, Tony decided to try to get aboard. He hailed the rather dozy looking rating standing in the conning tower of the submarine, said that he was a RN officer and demanded to be allowed to come aboard. He was politely asked to wait and the rating disappeared into the depths of the ship. He popped up again a couple of minutes later to tell Tony in a charming tone which indicated that he knew exactly what the latter was angling for, by saying "Not today, Sahib".

The college commandant was Major General Ranjit Singh, an Indian Cavalry officer of great dignity and charm. He epitomised the top ranks of the Indian military services, an officer of an army at the time the fourth largest after the USA, Russia and China, one amongst men of calibre and intelligence who had on many occasions since 1947 had to pull the chestnuts out of the fire for their political masters, who had allowed situations to develop that should have been avoided. That said, India is a vast country, composed of many different and opposed religions and sects, with some of the poorest people on earth, bound by superstitions and practices which won't allow for modernisation, and where the infrastructure of the nation always seems near to breaking point. To my mind after a year in the country it always seemed a miracle that anything worked at all but it invariably did, thanks to a system of government based upon the British model with a civil service and armed forces which always rose to the challenge when required. It was a wonderful experience to see all this at first hand.

Life in 1970 was not all about my military studies. The social routine of the college was fairly predictable with curry lunches and dances at the Gymkhana Club and team games in which some of the more athletic took part. I did not make much of a mark but Rosa did, playing tennis in various competitions, trying her hand at golf and riding with the Ooty Hounds, a local pack which hunted but never caught jackal on the Nilgiri Downs. The master of the hunt was a magnificent Indian Naval officer – in fact the Head of the Naval wing of the College called Captain Awati – a man with a flowing beard who took his responsibilities as seriously as any master of foxhounds in the English shires. When we eventually left Rosa arranged for the Cotswold Hunt to send a bitch in whelp to Wellington in an attempt to inject a new line into the local pack, an action much appreciated by Awati and his team. The hound travelled by Air India and arrived safely.

Nicholas and Hughie with Rosa's point to point winner's cup.

Tony and Susie Wilks.

Tony Wilks lived in the College Officers Mess, an existence which brought him into contact with a number of his fellow students whom he might not otherwise have got to know, but which meant that his predominantly Indian diet sometimes became a little irksome. Happily for him and also for Rosa and me, he met Susie Reed, the daughter of an English couple, long domiciled in India, who lived outside Bangalore where they bred and trained racehorses. Previously the Reeds had lived in Madras where Susie's father had worked in insurance. Susie was great fun and on return to Britain Tony and she married, something which pleased everyone who knew them. Sadly Tony died in 2005 at the age of sixty-nine after enduring a cruelly disfiguring cancer, far too young for a man of his abilities which covered everything you can think of: sailing, the Navy, travel, the piano, the stage – in 1970 he took the lead part in the Staff College play *"Boeing, Boeing"* alongside three of the prettiest Indian officers' wives – and the sights and sounds of wherever he happened to be or whatever he was involved in. A truly good friend and a fine example of a Royal Naval officer. He became one of Rosa's and my greatest friends and happily we still see a lot of Susie; their son Rupert is my godson.

We travelled whenever we could which was usually in the short breaks between the College's six academic terms or at the end of the course before returning home. We were lucky to have Gracie who looked after Nicholas and Hughie in our absence and who was totally dependable. The first long week end of the course we decided to go to Sri Lanka or Ceylon as it then was, which meant driving almost two hundred miles to Trichinopoly to catch a flight. So unaware were we of the potential dangers of such a journey that we had little idea of where to find our hotel or the airport and ended up driving down the main street at nine o'clock at night through a tight throng of people. When I later recounted this experience to Som Somana he gave me a tremendous rocket, telling me that if I had run anybody down we would probably both have been lynched with questions only being asked later. He advised me to carry a pistol if we were ever foolish enough to undertake such an ill-conceived journey again!

On another occasion we went with the Hamilton Russells to Kashmir, staying in a houseboat on the lovely Nageen lake. Kashmir was then, and still is, divided between India and Pakistan, neither country being able to reach agreement on its status which has been under dispute since 1947. It is a great sadness since the lakes and valleys in the foothills of the Himalayas, with Nanga Parbat, the ninth highest mountain in the world, towering above, presented a most magnificent spectacle. Our houseboat was comfortable, we swam in the lake the waters of which were not quite as clean as might have been wished, rode on horses up to the UN Cease Fire line – the only one of us not allowed off the leading rein by her groom was Rosa, the most gifted rider amongst the four of us – admired the wonderful gardens of Srinagar, the capital, and generally had a marvellous break from Wellington. Sadly today international rivalries have made Kashmir even harder to visit and I am told that, for climatic reasons, many of the lakes have dried out.

Nageen Lake, Kashmir.

Post course reunion at West Green Cottage.

It was a good year and I like to think we made the most of it. We learnt about an important nation, met some very impressive people including amongst my fellow students, saw some wonderful sights and accumulated a host of memories. In November the time came to leave Wellington and to say good bye to many good friends as well as to Muthu, Gracie and Fatima who had served us so well and to hand the faithful Triumph Herald back to Dr Munu. We spent the last fortnight of our time touring Northern India with Tony Wilks visiting Sikkim, Darjeeling, Delhi and Rajasthan before heading to Bombay. We finally left from there at the end of November with dear Gracie at the airport to wave us off.

Northern Ireland.

In 1968 the tensions long present in the island of Ireland boiled over once again, although they had been simmering below the surface ever since the division of the island into the Irish Republic and the British province of Northern Ireland, which had taken place in 1917. The history of the enmity between Protestants and Roman Catholics is well known, although the open dissension which arose after 1968, fuelled by extremists on both sides, brought those differences of religion, culture, belief and future aspirations into sharp focus once more. From the beginning of this latest outbreak of civil disobedience, rioting and eventually armed conflict, the British Army was deployed to attempt to keep the peace by separating the two sides, although whatever action soldiers might take was usually seen as partisan by one side or the other. This was the situation with which Rosa and I were met when we returned home to Britain from India in late 1970.

However, my posting on return from India was to Headquarters 3rd Division based at Bulford Camp on Salisbury Plain. I was appointed to be the Grade Two staff officer responsible for Operations and Organisation and I had three more junior officers to assist me: Joe Charlesworth, John Milne Hume and Mike Pethybridge. My boss was Colonel Barry Pollard, a Royal Engineer and the GOC was initially General Glyn Gilbert, later followed by Dick Worsley. The Division's role was to be prepared to act in concert with the RN amphibious force and RAF 38 Group to deploy to undertake interventionist operations wherever the United Kingdom Government decided that might be justified. In theory we might have been deployed overseas anywhere in the world although in practice, anyway in my time, we went nowhere, although I once accompanied Glyn Gilbert to an interesting exercise involving the Americans in the Virgin Islands. It was absorbing work planning for contingencies alongside clever and interesting people from all three services.

I earlier mentioned my enjoyment of Salisbury Plain when I was based there in 1960 and Rosa and I equally enjoyed our eighteen months 'on the plain' ten years later. We had a quarter on the outskirts of Bulford Camp just below the large chalk 'Kiwi' emblem dug out of the hillside by New Zealand troops at the end of the First World War, in order to keep them occupied and out of mischief before they could be returned home. The resulting work is not unlike the various white horses excavated at sites on chalkland in various parts of England. It was good to be based in Southern England for a while and, being only an hour and a half from Witcombe, we managed to see a lot of Rosa's family and other friends. However, the highlight was the birth of Willie at the Military Hospital in Tidworth at the end of May 1972.

I was due to remain with 3rd Division until December 1972 but in late July that year the 2nd Battalion of the regiment was ordered to make an emergency deployment to Northern Ireland along with a number of other units; the ostensible reason for such a sudden increase in operational force levels in the Province was to eliminate the IRA's control of the so-called 'no go' areas in the hard Republican parts of Belfast and Londonderry, areas where the Nationalist communities had for some months barricaded the streets and imposed their own authority. However, the 2nd Battalion had only recently been reformed after a period of 'suspended animation' or temporary disbandment and Tony Boam, the recently appointed CO, had no second in command. As a result, I was removed early from my staff job at Bulford and sent to Ulster to join the battalion, while Michael Thomson, a KOSB officer, my already appointed successor at 3rd Division and an old friend, had to move to Bulford somewhat earlier than he expected.

This sudden change of plan also scuppered some domestic aspirations. Willie's christening had been arranged and had to be postponed, while we had recently bought a house near Hartley Wintney in Hampshire and were in the process of finalising the purchase. As a result, Rosa found herself having to pack up and handover our married quarter at Bulford and move everything to West Green Cottage, arrange new schools for the children and take charge of numerous other activities, more properly the role of a husband. As expected she coped brilliantly and there were no hitches. It was the sort of situation that many Army wives will have encountered during their married lives.

Sectarian symbolism in Londonderry.

The second in command of any organisation is just that: not the boss but prepared and able to take over the top job if circumstances might demand that he should. There was little likelihood that over the four months we were in Londonderry, Tony would falter and only when he went on a few days leave, did I get my hands on the levers of power. However, there were aspects of the battalion's role that were handed to me for oversight or management. Our initial deployment was in the centre of Londonderry but after a few weeks we were given an extended area of operations which included the hardcore republican areas of the Bogside and the Shantallow to the north of the city. Johnny Clavering and Right Flank controlled the Brandywell; G Company under Richard Jenner Fust the walled city and the Bogside, with Robin Buchanan-Dunlop and Left Flank responsible for the Strand Road and Shantallow areas. Our role was to maintain law and order, to root out those republican elements intent upon disrupting life in the furtherance of their aspirations for a united Ireland and to restore some normality on the streets. They were exhausting and dangerous tasks with the ever-present threat of a bomb or a sniper attack, and sadly the battalion lost four soldiers killed in the course of their duties, but there was no doubt that by the time the battalion returned to Edinburgh in late November the level of violence had considerably reduced.

I was charged by Tony with handling community relations in the battalion's area and this involved trying to establish a dialogue with local people who were prepared to talk with the security forces to find common ground. I remember enlisting the help of Bill Jones, our Church of Scotland chaplain and Father John Williams, a Roman Catholic padre attached for the tour and between the three of us we tried to establish a rapport with people; at about the same time a group of five women from the Bogside, later dubbed the 'Peace Ladies', had got together to confront the IRA and to offer a different view to the authorities in London and Dublin as to how 'the troubles' might be brought to an end or at least reduced in the interests of those living locally. They were a feisty lot and we had interesting contacts with them but sadly they achieved little of substance in the end, a shame since they were genuinely motivated by a desire for peace, if at times rather naïve about the underlying purposes of the IRA's campaign to reunite the Irish people.

After return to Scotland the battalion moved south in the New Year to Pirbright in Surrey from where it was to undertake public duties. My circumstances also changed and I ceased to be second in command, handing that role to John Arthur, and took command of Right Flank from Johnny Clavering. For me it proved a very fortuitous move since I was once again commanding soldiers at the coalface and had another excellent team to support me: Simon Rose was my second in command and the three platoons were commanded by Henry Llewellyn, John Treadwell and Colour Sergeant Dick Freeman while CSM Syd Carnegie and CQMS John Crewe administered us all. I like to think it was a happy company and for me it brought about the establishment of an enduring friendship with Syd Carnegie, a man of enormous integrity and utterly dependable, later commissioned in the regiment and who now lives in Perth. He and his wife Dewnea are very good chums.

DMN and Syd Carnegie.

In November 1973, the battalion was once again deployed to Northern Ireland, this time to the hard republican areas of West Belfast to undertake security duties not dissimilar to those which had occupied it a year earlier in that part of Londonderry west of the river Foyle. Right Flank was assigned to the Ballymurphy – New Barnsley area, a part of the city with an uncompromising attitude to republicanism and a thirst for violence. The company was based in the Vere Foster School which had been taken over for the duration of the Northern Ireland military deployment (although some teaching still continued), a not uncomfortable base which had been protected with corrugated iron defences and sandbag emplacements to keep it secure against IRA rocket or sniper attack. During that tour we had plenty to occupy us and much to their credit, the guardsmen of Right Flank held their nerve against the taunts and physical attacks directed against them and I would like to think we left the area in March 1974 a better place than when we arrived four and a half months earlier. Twenty years later after I had left the Army I had the satisfying task of completing a history of the regiment covering the period 1956 to 1993; that history gives an insight into how both battalions of the Scots Guards conducted their various tours of duty over the years of violence that erupted in Ulster from 1968 and continued into the early years of the next century. All who served over that long period can be proud of their achievements.

Spring 1974 saw a return to Pirbright, another Queen's Birthday parade and in May a change of command when Colonel James Dunsmure took over from Tony Boam. The latter had had a very successful period in command bringing the battalion through two tours in Northern Ireland, having at the outset had to re-form it to undertake operational duties at next to no notice.

Rosa and Nicholas at West Green Cottage.

During this period with the battalion, Rosa and I lived at West Green Cottage, a fifteen mile commute to Pirbright. It was a joy to have a relatively undisturbed period living in our own house and able to undertake a reasonably normal life. The flexibility of army life in peacetime and how it permits the combining of military duties with a predominantly civilian existence 'out of hours', is an indication of how the British Army attempts to treat its people in order to provide them with a balanced lifestyle, so essential if they are to remain committed but content. For us this was important since all three boys were by then at Wellesley House prep school in Thanet or were about to go there, while later Nicholas and Hughie were to start at Cheltenham College and

William was to attend Grenville College near Bideford. These were choices made by Rosa and me and neither of us ever entertained any doubts that they were the right ones in each case; my father's generation and indeed some of my own contemporaries would no doubt have argued that my children should have been educated, if at all possible, where I myself had been regardless of whether or not that was best for the child concerned. I am afraid we didn't subscribe to such a position and are happy that we made the right decisions assisted by the wise counsels of people like their Wellesley House Headmaster, Bill Sale, a man of great common sense and humanity who, through marriage, happened to be well connected with Rosa's family. All this is in a real sense now academic but, judging by the way all three boys developed, how they used their University opportunities and what they have since made of life, I like to think we made the right decisions. We could not be prouder of them.

Late 1974 brought the news that I was to undertake another staff appointment, this time at Minden in Germany where I was to become the Brigade Major or Chief of Staff to the Commander 11th Armoured Brigade in 1st Division. This meant again leaving West Green Cottage, arranging for the house to be let and taking a ferry to the Continent. While professional soldiers are usually motivated by the demands and prospects of service life and while some postings are bound to be inconvenient, most servicemen would agree that you take such occurrences in your stride and get on with it; not necessarily so for their spouses, many of whom must sometimes have viewed another move to another married quarter, possibly in an unfamiliar overseas location, with foreboding. Never once did Rosa not accept where fate was to take us and always put heart and soul into the next move, accepting the need to go, to once more pack up our belongings and entrust our chosen home to others. I shall always remember my mother, who knew little of service life, asking Rosa when we were engaged whether she was ready and prepared 'to follow the drum'. She received an affirmative answer on that occasion and Rosa has held to it ever since.

My move to Minden brought me into contact with one of the kindest and most charming of officers that I ever met in my military service. Brigadier Mike Swindells, the Commander of 11th Armoured Brigade, was a man of great good sense and high standards, himself calm under pressure but equally able to motivate others into taking action when required. As I learnt on one occasion he had a quick temper – what his wife Prue described as an 'ink storm' – but they occurred rarely and were usually over in a flash. On the premise that you learn as much from those for whom you work by noting their example than you do from hours of study or reading, I think I learnt as much from Mike as I did from anybody in my military career. His death from drowning when swimming in the Mediterranean off Elba in 2016 was wretched and robbed those of us who knew and cherished him of a stalwart friend.

The role of the brigade was much the same as that of 4th Guards Brigade ten years previously. Little had changed in the way that NATO would have confronted a Soviet attack on Western Europe, although tactics and equipment had clearly been updated and altered to meet different battlefield scenarios. Minden was a medium sized German town well known as the point at which the river Weser flowing north intersected with the Mittelland Canal which flowed across Northern German from the Ruhr to Hanover. Rosa and I lived in a married quarter in the town amongst German neighbours, few of whom to our shame we got to know; learning German was not our forte although Rosa made more progress than I did. Years later when I was again serving in Germany I made a speech in German, at the end of which I was asked by one impertinent German if I was speaking in his language or French!

In Minden there were two Army couples of similar age to us who became very close friends but both of whose husbands later died very much before they should have. Peter Jones, a Royal Signals officer, was the senior administrator in the Brigade (as opposed to me as the Operations chief) and was married to Judith. He died not long after our time together of cancer, an undeserved and grievous death both for his family and the Army. He would have gone far. I am glad to say we remain in contact with Judith. The other family were the Lytles. Simon commanded the Army helicopter squadron in the Brigade and he and Pim had three sons of much the same ages as our own boys. We had a lot of fun with them and kept in touch thereafter; sadly, Simon died tragically about ten years ago for reasons which must remain a mystery but again we happily maintain contact with Pim and the family. Re-reading the words above it seems that Minden wasn't a very lucky place for us, losing as we did three such good friends for widely different reasons, long before their time should have come.

I only served just over a year of my allotted two years as Brigade Major when I was told I had been selected to command the 2nd Battalion Scots Guards in September 1976. For a regimental soldier such an appointment has to be the pinnacle of his career and for me it meant everything to have been selected to command the battalion in which I had served so much of my time in the regiment, and where I already knew so many people of all ranks. I therefore left Minden at the beginning of 1976, attended a number of courses designed to prepare me for regimental command and for three weeks in the summer helped out as the Commandant of the Royal Tournament at Earl's Court. Although the latter involved much hanging around late into the evening and became a trifle tedious as one viewed the same acts over and over again – the Royal Naval field gun race over an obstacle course being a good example – the tournament provided a great showpiece for the three armed services and it was sad when twenty years later it was axed as part of a programme of Government spending cuts.

2nd Battalion Scots Guards 1976-1979.

The battalion I was to command was by September 1976 based in Munster in Westphalia. James Dunsmure was in command and I took over from him at the end of the month with Rosa and I moving into the CO's house at 6a Angelesachen Weg. It was to be a very happy and a thoroughly worthwhile tour for both of us.

2SG was the military short hand for the 2nd Battalion and I shall use that abbreviation in this account; it was a mechanised battalion of around 600 soldiers with four companies and was part of the 2nd Division under the immediate local command of Brigadier Desmond Langley. The latter and General Frank Kitson, the Divisional Commander, were both very supportive of the battalion and we always knew where we stood with both. In a relatively small organisation like the British Army people tend to appear in one's life, then disappear, only to re-appear later, usually in a totally different place or context. Clearly this can sometimes be disadvantageous if the initial encounter has not been a success but it is generally beneficial and helps to boost confidence.

Birthday boy - Londonderry March 1977.

Certainly, I generally enjoyed meeting those previously served with. I always respected Frank Kitson, a wise if unconventional soldier, while Desmond was a most enjoyable and affable man.

Desmond Langley in Canada.

As a mechanised battalion we were equipped with an armoured personnel carrier called an FV 432. Each company would have had around fifteen such vehicles and their conceptual use broadly rested upon their deploying with armoured squadrons of Chieftain tanks to overrun and then consolidate an enemy position. Close co-operation between armour and mechanised infantry was therefore the basic tactic underpinning training for war and something always emphasised whenever we operated as a battle group.

Throughout the two and a half years I had command of 2SG I was admirably served by a succession of subordinates: Anthony Milner Brown; MIE Scott; Robin Buchanan-Dunlop; Kim Ross; Ewan Cameron; Iain MacKay-Dick; Jeremy Cox; Anthony Leask, Randall Nicol and Ian McLaughlan all commanded companies at some time or other while three of them were later elevated to be the battalion Second in Command. They were not just fellow officers but real friends as were Douglas Erskine Crum and Alec Ramsay, both of whom served as my Adjutant. Then there were others in more junior appointments, sadly too numerous to mention here.

The same was equally true of the senior members of the Sergeants Mess. RSM Jim Bunton, his drill sergeants and all the CSMs were already known to me and they and others lower down the chain of command within the battalion gave me dedicated and unstinting support. Here I would also include the Quartermasters: the Lawrie brothers and Clark Brown. Along with all the guardsmen, who constituted the bedrock of the battalion, I like to think we were a happy bunch and, because everybody pulled together, I believe we showed ourselves to be a professional and cohesive battalion, ready and able to do anything asked of us. Most importantly of all we enjoyed soldiering together.

Jim Bunton and Douglas Erskine Crum.

Life is full of challenges and usually the better and more enjoyable for that. By September 2SG was already preparing for a tour of duty in Northern Ireland, this time under command of 8th Brigade in Londonderry commanded by Brigadier Bryan Webster. We were to have responsibility for the hard republican areas west of the river Foyle including the Creggan and the Bogside, places which we knew well from the tour undertaken four years earlier. While the campaign being pursued by the IRA still had the same political objectives, their tactics had altered with the adoption of more sophisticated attacks and a growing tendency to try to draw the security forces into hostile situations known as 'come ons' rather than staging random confrontations as had happened previously. That did not mean that there was necessarily less violence, only that it was better orchestrated and usually accompanied by publicity designed to paint troops and police in a less than favourable light. We had therefore to be ready for anything and the guardsman on the street had to be extra aware as he patrolled, searched houses for weapons or suspects or, as was often necessary, arrested known or suspected terrorists for questioning, usually at the behest of the police. By 1976 under the terms of a political initiative called Police Primacy, the Royal Ulster Constabulary were once more leading the effort to bring the long running campaign of terrorist activity to an end. We, their military counterparts, worked closely with them sharing intelligence, operations rooms and other facilities, a most necessary step towards presenting a united front to those determined to overthrow the rule of law by whatever means.

Londonderry in winter is not the most inviting of places and dour, changeable weather and endless low-level patrolling often made for long periods of boredom, a potentially greater danger than a confrontation with the IRA, since once a man dropped his guard he inevitably became a soft target for the terrorist gunman. Thankfully we sustained no casualties and throughout tried our best to engage with the people of our area with but limited success. We eventually returned to Munster at the end of March knowing that, without involving itself in any headline events, 2SG had done a professional and worthwhile job in helping to keep the peace and restoring a degree of normality, in the process assisting in furthering the political processes without which in due course the violence would not have been brought to an end with the signing of the Good Friday agreement in 1998.

From 1977 until the battalion's eventual departure from Germany in Spring 1979, we trained for our war role as part of NATO's defensive structure prepared and equipped to counter any Soviet attack on members of the alliance in Western Europe. That training was conducted mainly within Germany with occasional exercises arranged for battalions or companies in host nations in Africa, Canada, the USA and the Middle East. One of these exercises involved the 2SG all arms battle group – a balanced unit of two armoured squadrons and two mechanised infantry companies – flying to Western Canada to train on the prairies at Suffield about two hundred miles east of Calgary. The training, using live ammunition provided an experience that in peacetime came as close as was possible to practising fire and manoeuvre on a realistic scale, utilising all the weaponry at the battle group commander's disposal. For me as the CO it was not unlike being the conductor of an orchestra. In August 1977 2SG was joined by an armoured squadron of the 'Skins' (the Inniskilling Dragoon Guards) and another from the Royal Tank Regiment while we had attached to us from the Canadian Armed Forces an armoured infantry company of the Princess Patricia's Canadian Light Infantry. The rest of the battle group was formed from 2SG with G Company under Ewan Cameron, while the Battle Group HQ and the logistic support were all Scots Guardsmen.

The Canadian prairie at dawn.

It proved a most worthwhile and enjoyable month of largely unrestricted training and people became more confident as they got used to handling tank guns, artillery and small arms on exercises contrived to permit a battle group's full potential as a fighting force, to be realised. It was undoubtedly one of the best training experiences to be provided to units in BAOR who had hitherto had to make do with increasingly restricted opportunities to train within Germany. I believe similar training continues in Canada to this day.

The battle group command vehicle. DMN, John Cargill and RSM Bunton.

Life for 2SG was not all military training and the battalion had a social life in Germany, sometimes of its own and sometimes shared with those units amongst which we lived in Munster. The latter was a sizeable, semi industrial German city with a history stretching back several centuries and included an ancient University. Almost totally obliterated in the Second World War the city had been painstakingly restored to its former glory, something the Germans managed with great skill. There were six major British Army units spread around the greater city area and generally speaking Anglo-German relations were good with tolerance being shown by all parties. That said over half a century of 'occupation' invariably led to strained relations from time to time.

A regiment or infantry battalion is very much a family and Rosa and I (and I deliberately include her) looked upon ourselves as the heads of that family. My role as the CO of the battalion and therefore responsible for the standards, behaviour and results achieved by my guardsmen will be obvious enough. On the other hand, Rosa's role was more indeterminate and, while the Wives' Club offered the means by which she could support and encourage the battalion's families, it was a very informal organisation and what was achieved happened only because of leadership and personality. Rosa was supported by Mary Bunton, the RSM's wife, and between them they managed to make life a little easier for the less confident families, some of whom had probably not been abroad before going to Germany and, on arrival, could find themselves living several miles from the barracks in a German town or village. We were lucky in that 2SG had a first-rate families support team led by Clark Brown and later Ewan Lawrie. Many people had much to thank the two of them for.

Rosa in the egg and spoon race at Munster.

Visits and get togethers were arranged from time to time to increase families' awareness of where they were, the reasons for our being based in Germany or what their husbands' professional roles involved. On one occasion Rosa and Mary arranged for the wives to be shown some of the equipment their husbands might have to use; all was well until one guardsman's wife got into the driver's seat of a 16 Tonne FV 432 APC but froze at the controls when instructed to turn in a different direction and ploughed into the side of a building. Luckily no one was hurt but considerable damage to the building occurred and at one stage it looked as if there would be some very embarrassing questions to answer. Fortunately, Brigadier Bill Woodburn, who had taken over command of the Garrison from Desmond Langley, had contacts in the world of military engineering and managed to square somebody to fix matters. Never have I been more grateful to my immediate superior!

Many families travelled across Europe for their holidays and Munster's relative proximity to the Baltic, the Alps and the South of France made travel easy. On my return from Londonderry Rosa and I took the three boys, plus two dogs, by car to near Narbonne in France where we picked up a cabin cruiser in order to travel along the Canal du Midi. It offered a wonderful prospect but the combination of the five of us, two dogs and two bicycles in a Renault 16, a decision to camp en route and, on arrival, to find the *Mistral* wind was blowing, made for an interesting and at moments a not entirely satisfactory experience! I learnt later that such was the deleterious effect that the *Mistral* could have upon people that it could be used as a defence in a case of murder! Despite some fairly testing moments, including negotiating the seven locks at Carcassonne in driving snow and finding most mornings that the condensation inside the boat caused our bedclothes to become wringing wet necessitating their having to be dried out in the oven, we survived and the final few days on the canal brought us beautiful weather. Maybe March was not a very good time to go on such a jaunt but at least we had the canal to ourselves apart from one other equally misguided British family! Years later after we had settled in North Yorkshire we met that family: they were the Worsleys from Hovingham and Marcus was by then the county's Lord Lieutenant. Small world!

Another event which gave us all great enjoyment was the presentation of new colours to the battalion in April 1978. Battalions in the British Army tend to receive colours every fifteen years or so depending upon how much use the colours may have experienced. Being a Foot Guards battalion meant that both the Queen's and Regimental Colours would have been frequently carried when the battalion was mounting Royal Duties in London; wear and tear could be quite marked after even a short period and new colours had therefore to be provided quite regularly. In our case 1978 was the ordained date for new ones to be presented. However, colours for Foot Guards battalions traditionally tend to be presented in Britain and then normally, anyway in the case of the Scots Guards, either at Buckingham Palace or at Holyroodhouse in Edinburgh. To some in the Household Division the prospect of a battalion parading in Germany or anywhere else overseas was not to be countenanced, and it was decreed that our parade should be postponed until 1979.

While that was the thinking in Horse Guards, we in Germany had a contrary view. First there was a precedent in that the 1st Battalion of the regiment had been presented with new colours at Pirbright in 1964 before departing for a tour of duty in Malaysia; secondly any parade in London in the spring of 1979 would have had to be fitted in to an already crowded ceremonial programme before the Queen's Birthday Parade that June, when the battalion was scheduled to troop its new Queen's Colour. Under the circumstances it would have been hard to engender the family ethos of a parade designed to harness the spirit of the battalion and its commitment to its monarch, if the parade was to be shoe horned into an already crowded ceremonial programme. As a result, Murray de Klee, Regimental Lieutenant Colonel at the time, made the case for the parade to be held in Germany in 1978 on the grounds that from the battalion's standpoint, it would provide a more enjoyable occasion and an opportunity to celebrate a successful tour in Germany, soon to be completed.

Presentation of Colours – Schloss Nordkirchen 1978.

The Queen having given her assent, Horse Guards reluctantly agreed and we chose Schloss Nordkirchen, a nineteenth century Schloss about twenty miles from Munster and formerly the palace of the Bishops of Munster, as the venue for the parade. The building, at the time a training establishment for German tax inspectors, was ideal for such an occasion and provided an imposing background for what turned out a most worthwhile and enjoyable day. The Colonel, the Duke of Kent, presented the colours on behalf of The Queen accompanied by Iain Ferguson, by then the Regimental Lieutenant Colonel, with many of 'the great and good' of BAOR gathered to witness a very special day for the battalion. Parties were held over the next few days and we all thoroughly enjoyed ourselves. The decision to hold the parade was seen to be fully justified by those serving in 2SG!

There was however a sequel to all this, anyway for me! As already mentioned the battalion was to leave Munster in early April to move to Chelsea Barracks to be based alongside the 1st Battalion of the regiment, an event which happens very infrequently, and to then troop its recently presented Queen's Colour on the 1979 Queen's Birthday Parade. It had been my hope that I would be allowed to remain in command until after the Troop in mid-June before reporting to the Staff College at Camberley, where I was to become an instructor on the Directing Staff of the college. However before leaving Germany I was informed that the Staff College wanted me earlier than planned and that I should therefore hand over command of 2SG to Johnny Clavering in mid-May; as might be expected this was a disappointment since to command the Queen's Birthday parade is amongst the highest of honours for a guardsman. Whether I would have done it well is another matter but I would certainly have jumped at the chance; imagine my further irritation when on arrival at Camberley and in conversation with Brigadier Alastair Dennis, the Deputy Commandant, I discovered that there had been no request for me to arrive there earlier. I suspect that Horse Guards, irritated at 2SG's success in being allowed to hold their Colours parade in Germany, were determined to pay back the promoter of the original request!

Leaving the Battalion for the last time. Chelsea Barracks 1979.

Iain Ferguson commanded the parade in my stead and I handed over command of the battalion in mid-May after two and a half wonderful years serving with people for whom I still have enormous regard and affection. Thereafter I would never again serve directly with Scots Guardsmen although I might encounter them in the course of later appointments in the Army. However, before I close this account of my life within the regiment I must mention two people who worked for Rosa and me in Munster: Lance Corporal Harry Shuttleworth, my orderly, and Lance Corporal Dennis Wray, my staff car driver. Both helped us enormously and Dennis in particular remains a good pal. Interestingly when twenty years later we bought Minster Hill, our house in North Yorkshire, we were looking for a reliable electrician when Dennis, whom we did not know was by then living and working in York, was recommended by a close local friend, Nicholas Shepherd. The rest can be guessed but another thirty years on Dennis and his son Alastair still come to do jobs for us when needed. A truly happy outcome.

Chapter Four

Military Life after the Regiment 1979-1992

1979-1981.

T his period in my life covered a number of service appointments, mainly in Britain. For much of the time we were able to live in our own house, initially at West Green although in 1981 we bought one half of the manor house in the village of South Warnborough, a couple of miles south of Odiham and not far from Alton. The move was necessitated by a growing family and the need for more space including for Rosa's horses, requirements which South Warnborough Manor provided to a tee. We occupied the south side of the building with a couple called Carpenter the other end and a third family, the Taylors, in the old stables. The various conversions had been done only a few years before and we undoubtedly had the best of the changes. Early on we filled in the rather unattractive and troublesome swimming pool and built a tennis court in the garden, both changes which we came to enjoy. St Andrew's Church dating from the early twelfth century was just over the fence so we could walk there on a Sunday. The only drawback was the busy A32 road which ran through the village and, although later downgraded, it still remains as busy as ever.

By the time we arrived in South Warnborough, Nicholas had left Wellesley House and moved to Cheltenham College for five years. Richard Morgan, a highly regarded and very approachable headmaster, who in time went on to become the Warden at Radley, and Richard Kent, a former Royal Navy officer and the housemaster of Newick House, were responsible for guiding him through the latter stages of his education and Rosa and I will always be grateful for the trouble they took to see him through his formative years. In due course Hughie joined Nick at Cheltenham but, in the meantime, Willie and he were still at Wellesley House, growing in confidence and stature under the watchful eye of Bill and Tessa Sale.

South Warnborough.

Our time in Hampshire allowed us to indulge in some of the pastimes which both Rosa and I had been brought up to enjoy in our younger days. She rode and hunted with the Hampshire Hunt, I shot – mainly at Witcombe – and we played tennis and met local people, mostly in the village, such as Andy and Jean Young, Douglas and Elizabeth Harris and the Forbes. We also consolidated some old friendships from earlier military times with people with whom I had served like Bill and Margaret Stanford at Froyle and

Nicholas shooting for Cheltenham at Bisley. With Rosa and Willie.

Andrew and Romy Parsons, the latter Scots Guards friends from a long way back. Generally speaking though we didn't make as many friends in Hampshire as we might have done; whether this was because we were only there for short periods between postings or because the northern half of the county was generally orientated towards London commuting with many people only coming home at week-ends, I don't know. Indeed, on those occasions when I later worked in the MOD in Central London I became a commuter from Winchfield to Waterloo myself. However, Hampshire proved an enjoyable place to live and we did make some new friends, most notably Christopher and Jane Baker near Odiham. Christopher, a Lloyds underwriter and like me a railway enthusiast, and I planned many a railway expedition in years afterwards, including taking our wives across Canada by train and then by boat up to Alaska to travel the 'gold rush' line from Skagway before sailing into Glacier Bay, a memorable trip. A few years later we all flew to Italy to travel with a group of fellow enthusiasts along the rural railways of Tuscany. This involved Italian Railways providing a steam locomotive and some ancient rolling stock to convey us through wonderful countryside, allowing us to stop when we wanted to take photographs or, when we reached a suitable place, to alight for lunch. Christopher and I were in our element while Rosa and Jane, sitting demurely in one corner of our carriage doing their knitting, quietly tolerated our child-like behaviour. They weren't quite so tolerant when, for the umpteenth time the carriage filled with smoke as we went through yet another tunnel, and Christopher and I were too slow in raising the compartment windows! It was however a lovely trip for us all and we visited Florence, Assisi. Pisa and Lucca.

Travelling across Canada with the Bakers in 2003. Scrabble in the dome car!

Steam in Tuscany. The crew were probably Mafia supporters!

Lunch break!

One aspect of owning our own house at West Green Cottage and later at South Warnborough, was the need to let them when I was posted overseas. Many wives might have used home ownership as a reason not to accompany their husbands but not Rosa. In all we let on half a dozen occasions using a rather moderate agency in Farnham to find a suitable tenant and manage the let; invariably the agency always seemed inclined to favour the tenant rather than the landlord. We had one or two good tenants – namely the Duffs when we were at West Green and later the Mogers at South Warnborough – but some of the others were less satisfactory. We also had one or two disasters which could not be attributed to tenants; in January 1982 just after we had departed for our fourth tour in Germany, the pipes in the Manor froze and water cascaded down the staircase doing quite a bit of damage. Fortunately, Andy and Jean Young were on hand to come to the rescue which was very good of them.

The second half of 1979 saw me as an instructor at the Staff College. My role along with a number of other lieutenant colonels was to assist in preparing officers of the rank of major and captain for their future careers in the Army, a sort of year long 'university course' similar to that which I had attended in India nine years previously. I had two basic responsibilities: first to teach a group of up to ten students by means of written exercises, practical out door tactical discussions – known as TEWTs or Tactical Exercises Without Troops – and round table discussions in the classroom. My second task was to be a member of a 'think tank' team covering an aspect of warfare that British troops might conceivably become involved in, such as European Warfare or Counter Insurgency operations. Knowledge gained from my time serving in BAOR and in Northern Ireland helped and I quite enjoyed such work; I got particular satisfaction from writing an exercise for the College codenamed 'Tidal Wave' which was devised to address and solve the tactical and political issues which arose from the need to control the annual 12th August Apprentice Boys March in Londonderry. The Apprentice Boys, a strongly supported society in parts of Britain and Canada originally formed in 1814 derived from the siege of Londonderry in 1688/9 when the forces of James II attempted to invest the city causing thirteen apprentice boys to close the city gates. The parade in the latter half of the twentieth century sadly often degenerated into rioting and communal violence.

Inevitably the presence of a large number of ambitious officers in one place at Camberley – both those teaching and those being taught – led to the generation of a hot house atmosphere; happily, I was able to live at West Green and so escaped there when not needed. After a year I was promoted to Colonel and was selected for another appointment. I was not sad to move on, although sorry to leave behind good friends like Michael Thomson, Simon Lytle, Nick Ansell, Christopher Wolverson and others.

The original plan was for me to go to command the All Arms Tactics Wing of the School of Infantry at Warminster in Wiltshire. For some reason there was no suitable house for us there and so we decided to take up the offer of renting the Old Rectory at Fovant near Wilton which was reasonably close. The house was on part of the Morrison family's estate and was owned by Sarah Morrison who had two brothers, both MPs. Before we appeared on the scene another Army officer had rented the house so the Morrisons seemed fairly relaxed about continuing the association with the military. I remember Rosa and I being summoned to Sarah's flat in Pimilco to be interviewed, a cursory and enjoyable experience which took minutes before we hit the bottle in mutual celebration! The prospect of living in such a lovely part of England was exciting although we were sad at once again having to leave our own house.

However, this plan came to nothing since at the last moment my posting to Warminster was changed and I was ordered instead to report for a job on the Defence Policy Staff in the MOD Main Building in Whitehall. The policy staff reported directly to the Chief of the Defence Staff through a series of directors of whom Air Commodore David Parry-Evans, a relaxed but ambitious former bomber pilot, was to be my immediate boss. The other two members of the tri-service team were David Jackson, a very pleasant RAF group captain and Captain Garth de Courcy Ireland of the Navy. We were supposed to be a defence 'global think tank' which could come up with military solutions to problems posed by the UK's wish to maintain certain strategic interests around the world; however, we each had the contradictory role of also representing our own single service interests in any particular situation, a role which put us under pressure from our single service chiefs and their staffs and which often led to difficult debates within our own ranks. It was a time when pressure from the Treasury was exposing the practices and future requirements of the three services in an often unflattering light; no service was keen to concede the loss of a capability or manpower and so the arguments tended to be endless and often nugatory, and the inter service politics sometimes cruel.

I was lucky in that the Chief of the General Staff was General Dwin Bramall, a widely respected, highly capable and friendly man. I found him a delight to deal with and he pulled my chestnuts out of the fire on more than one occasion. However, the pressures were constant and not all of us survived. Garth de Courcy Ireland experienced a rough ride from the Navy Department who were apt to summon him downstairs for what the rest of us came to call 'a dark blue rinse' when they insisted on telling him what they thought must be included in any papers we were about to write; in the end they concluded that he was not serving their best interests, replacing him overnight without consultation with David Parry-Evans, with a thrusting naval captain, Nick Hill-Norton, being nominated as his successor. Nick was more the sort of man the Navy wanted since he possessed considerable confidence and not a little aggression and, being the son of a widely feared Admiral father who had been Chief of the Defence Staff in his day, gave the immediate impression of knowing most of the answers to the numerous problems faced by the three services at the time. The fact that most of the proposed solutions from his service department seemed to favour the Navy didn't appear to worry Nick; however, he could be charming and we got along alright and I still see him occasionally, if staying with Andrew and Romy Parsons at Newton Valence where Nick also now lives.

So my time on the policy staff was not a lot of fun. It was my first experience of serving in a Government department and the combination of an unpleasant working environment, unappealing tasks, long hours and commuting made for a less than happy fifteen months. One of our few pleasures was when the Chief of the Defence Staff, Admiral Terry Lewin, would descend from his sixth floor office to come and discuss some of the issues of the day with us. A man of enormous charm and impressive stature he immediately put those junior to him at their ease; I can recall the three of us and David Parry-Evans sitting with him, often with a glass of sherry or whisky in our hands, having thoroughly sensible discussions. I don't suppose we probably stopped to think how much more difficult life must have been for him who had constantly to deal with politicians and senior civil servants; the Defence Secretary at the time was one John Nott who in Summer 1981 went on holiday to the Caribbean and returned having lain on the beach and sketched out on the back of an envelope his preferred plans for the future direction of the armed forces. Luckily for the latter, in particular the Royal Navy, the Falkland Islands war intervened the following year, consigning most of John Nott's wilder flights of strategic fantasy to the bin! I think Margaret Thatcher later sacked him.

22nd Armoured Brigade 1982-1983.

My time on the policy staff was brought to an earlier conclusion than might have been expected when, in Summer 1981, the Army published the list of those who were to be promoted to brigadier or one star rank the following year, including those who had been selected to command brigades. Along with Nick Ansell, Patrick Brooking and Peter Davies who were all destined to command brigades in BAOR, I was appointed to take over 22nd Armoured Brigade based at Hohne in Lower Saxony. I was to follow Robert Ward, a QDG, in January 1982.

Hohne is hard to identify since there is no civilian settlement with that name marked on today's maps, no doubt for good reason. The notorious Belsen-Bergen wartime concentration camp is less than five kilometres from the nearby former German barracks in Hohne which, after 1945, became a base for a brigade and some supporting troops of BAOR's forces positioned close to the Inner German Border. We visited the Belsen Camp on several occasions, mainly to allow visitors to see the place and to be reminded of the horrors of the Nazi culture and its ideological plans for a future civilisation, which resulted in the incarceration and subsequent deaths of countless people of so many different races and nationalities at Belsen and other camps in Nazi occupied Europe between 1940 and 1945. It was sobering to reflect on the human behaviour which had allowed the creation of such a place in an age when most people might have imagined mankind had put the practices which occurred, firmly behind it. The horror of the place remained in one's mind for a long time after studying the detailed photographs and the reconstruction of some buildings, all displayed to ensure that what had occurred there should never be forgotten. More than anything else it was very noticeable that one never heard birdsong in the vicinity of Belsen; that really made a lasting impression.

Celle.

I felt enormous satisfaction but not a little trepidation on being appointed to command 22nd Armoured Brigade. Satisfaction in that I was to be promoted against some fairly serious competition and trepidation in that I was to have nearly 5,000 officers and soldiers under command with, potentially, enormous operational responsibilities. During my time the composition of the brigade changed but ultimately it was designated a 'square' brigade with two armoured regiments – the 14th/20th Hussars and 2nd Royal Tank Regiment – and two armoured infantry battalions – the 1st Royal Anglian Regiment followed later by the 3rd Royal Green Jackets, and the 2nd Coldstream Guards – with various supporting arms like artillery, field engineers and logistic services. These units were stationed in places like Celle, a lovely and very picturesque German town, Fallingbostel and Hildesheim. Hohne was on the eastern fringes of the Luneberger Heide, an attractive area of heathland upon which NATO units practised fire and movement and where artillery and other heavy weapon systems were fired.

The difference between commanding a battalion of one's own soldiers whom one knew well and with whom one had much in common and being responsible for a number of hitherto unknown units, each of which had its own ethos and customs which should be respected and not trespassed upon unless there were good grounds for doing so, will need no elaboration. In short the Brigadier needed to step carefully to avoid unnecessarily treading on sensitive toes and inflaming prejudices for no good purpose but, equally he should be prepared to demand improvements and conformity when needed; I did have one unit whose reputation amongst my superiors for maintaining less than adequate operational standards and for adopting a sometimes unprofessional approach to soldiering was the subject of considerable comment but, by the time we parted company after two years, matters had improved. Another unit in the Brigade which at the time clearly felt that I was too strict with them, produced a T shirt emblazoned with the words 'I have been Naylor-ed' presumably indicating that I had been unnecessarily hard on them at some stage. I took it as a compliment!

Amongst my COs were people who became good friends: Peter Harman and Mike Tennant in Hohne; Richard Macfarlane in Fallingbostel; Roger Ker and later Christopher Wallace in Celle; also Ian Fowler in Celle and Simon Lytle, sadly now dead, and Tony Stone in Hildesheim. They were all easy to deal with and I like to think we generally got along well together without getting up each other's noses too often! In addition to commanding the operational units of the brigade I also had responsibility for a number of Garrison units in the same places, some of which did not come under my command operationally. The peacetime system of command in Germany had grown up over a long number of years and after a while mal-location had inevitably occurred leading to a sometimes muddled web of responsibilities; there were no problems so long as commanders understood the system and avoided getting in each other's way.

My HQ of a dozen officers was well knit and I like to think effective. Merrick Willis, a Queensman, and later Andrew Gadsby from the RTR, were respectively my chief of staff or Brigade Major while Mike Raworth headed the logistic branches in the HQ. All did me well and without their loyal support I would have had a far less relaxed two years in command. I was also fortunate to have good relations with those higher up the chain of command. Brian Kenny, the Divisional Commander at Verden, was one of the kindest and nicest officers I ever had the good fortune to serve under. A cavalryman with long experience of armoured soldiering he took enormous trouble to understand those who served him and was unfailingly loyal and considerate to all ranks; he was a fine sportsman and he and his wife Diana were always welcome visitors to Hohne. Further up the ladder was Nigel Bagnall, the Corps Commander, a no nonsense general with a deserved reputation for not tolerating fools, who concentrated on maintaining the highest standards of operational readiness across his command and who accepted nothing less – often to the dismay of the unwary – but who was always unfailingly kind and courteous. Finally, there was the Army Commander or C in C far way at Rheindahlen near the Dutch border. One of the holders of that appointment during my two years in Hohne was Michael Gow, my erstwhile CO in Kenya twenty years earlier when I served as his Adjutant!

Brian Kenny and James Rucker at Hohne.

I have already described life in Germany for those serving within NATO. Little had changed since Rosa and I first went there in 1965, although the more senior I became, the more I came to understand and became more closely associated with the civic and administrative structure of the country in which we were living. I dealt with the Burgermeisters and Stadtdirectors of the towns within my area and also met a number of senior citizens who were invariably friendly and easy to deal with. However, the original reasons underpining 'occupation' were increasingly coming to be questioned, particular so when NATO troops exercised over German countryside and farmers' land. Troops had to train and practice deployment and that was understood, but even so increasingly onerous 'rules' for the conduct of training tended to render the value of many manoeuvres questionable, especially when the economic costs of the damage done to infrastructure and agricultural land came to be assessed. In 1983 the end of 'occupation' – although obviously no one knew it at the time – was only six years away when the Berlin Wall came down, leading to the re-unification of Germany and the eventual staged return of British and other NATO forces to their own countries. Looking back, I marvel at the way the German population accepted the presence and activities of so many foreign soldiers over nearly fifty years.

With brother Christopher at Hopp House.

My ability to speak German was never very praiseworthy and there were several occasions when I was put to shame by Rosa. The trouble was that, however hard I tried to converse in their language, German acquaintances always countered in their far better English which they were understandably keen to improve. The inevitable result was that I and other British officers invariably took the easy way out and spoke in English. I always admired people like Brian Kenny who mastered German which must have given him enormous satisfaction and garnered him respect from the Germans.

We had to entertain a number of people while living in the Brigadier's house and Hopp House was very suitable for the purpose. Most of our guests were from within the brigade but people, mainly family, came to stay. The house was a solidly built, comfortable residence which in some ways looked not unlike a barrack block but we and the boys enjoyed our time there visiting those parts of Germany not visited on previous tours. Places like Hanover and the Harz Mountains were quite close and several times we travelled to Berlin from Helmstedt through the Soviet Zone on the famous British military train, which by virtue of the post-war Quadripartite Agreement between the allies and the Russians, had to run virtually every day of the year. It was an exciting journey with dogs being run along the tracks beneath the train before the journey started to ensure there were no stowaways hiding under the carriages, while no fraternisation with the Russians and the East Germans was permitted. The latter always tried to strike up conversations in order to show that we should deal with them rather than the Russians, thereby placing them on an equal footing with the three Western occupying powers. The Russians were allegedly fiendishly difficult to deal with and any mistake in official documentation, such as a full stop in the wrong place, was jumped upon as an infringement of the rules for the transit of their zone of occupation to Berlin and, if they felt so minded, an excuse to delay the train's departure in order to be tiresome.

Being as close as we were, we also visited the Inner German border between the two halves of the country, a depressing experience as one gazed upon miles of fencing, barbed wire entanglements, Alsatian dogs running on fixed static lines, searchlights and watchtowers stretching as far as the eye could see and all manned by morose looking Russian or East Germany personnel. The fence ran from the Baltic to the Swiss frontier. As a left over from the partitioning of Germany in 1945 the Inner German Border was patrolled where it was co-terminus with the British zone, by police who had their origins in Royal Naval personnel serving at that time in Hamburg. They still wore naval uniform and were led by a jovial and interesting man called Jack Bell.

Although we were in a foreign country, we led a pretty normal English life in Hohne. Rosa took her hunter, Cuckoo, with her – hunting on occasions with a local German pack of bloodhounds – and we had Nethy, the first of six spaniels to subsequently grace the Naylor household over a number of decades. The boys, when back from school, had their bicycles and other treasured possessions and made local friends. Despite Hohne being one of the least inspiring of places with its insalubrious connections to the last war, distasteful both to many Germans and not a few British families, the Naylors actually quite enjoyed their two years there and were in many ways sorry to leave. However, the British Army posting system depends on moving its subjects around at regular intervals and after two years I was due another move. In late 1983 I was told that I was to go to the Royal College of Defence Studies in London to attend the 1984 course. This was good news in that it meant a year at home living at South Warnborough and again getting to know that area of Hampshire. I therefore handed over command of 22nd Armoured Brigade to Mike Wilkes, an SAS soldier, in December and prepared for a sabbatical year at the RCDS.

Prime Ministerial visit.

Towards the end of my time in command, Margaret Thatcher made a prime ministerial visit to BAOR, allegedly to stiffen our sinews lest we might be going 'wobbly'. Hohne Garrison was selected to play a small part in the visit and I had to host her when she visited the local British primary school.

Dwin Bramall, by then Chief of the Defence Staff, accompanied her and at one juncture told me to offer her the chance to use the loo before her next engagement, which was to ride on a tank across the training area. As I was accompanying the Prime Minister around the school I therefore indicated to her that, should she wish to avail herself of the opportunity there was a loo just ahead of us, at which she stopped, turned to me and said, "Dear boy, when you have electioneered as long as I have, you learn to do without the loo!"

During our various tours in Germany we became very familiar with travelling to the Continent. Crossing by ferry – usually from Dover to Zeebrugge or the Hook of Holland – and driving along interminable miles of autobahn became second nature, but it was a tiring and often depressing journey when returning from a home leave. The arrangements for moving belongings or furniture were very efficiently managed by the Military Forwarding Organisation but it all required time and effort and I am glad we no longer have to do it. Much more of a saga was conveying animals back and forth; for dogs it was relatively straightforward there being no option but to 'air freight' them back to quarantine kennels in Britain where they would languish for six months until judged to be free from incubating rabies. Horses were another matter altogether. I think Rosa took a horse to Germany twice: the first occasion returning from Munster we failed to get the EU documentation for the movement of animals right and had a major confrontation with the Belgian shipping agents at Zeebrugge. I can recall arriving back at West Green at 5 o'clock the next morning after a second confrontation over documentation and a demand that we pay VAT on Cuckoo with the Dover Port authorities, both of us totally exhausted! Returning from Hohne four years later we were better organised and Rosa and Willie were booked to travel from Hamburg to Hull; sod's law however intervened and forecast bad weather dictated the horse could not travel, so they had to return to Hohne before setting out again several days later!

I wonder whether husbands who served in Germany always appreciated the wonderful support they received from their wives. As previously mentioned I recall when Rosa and I were engaged, my mother asking her whether she was really happy 'to follow the drum' receiving a very affirmative response. Her loyal and loving support over years travelling to both well known and sometimes hardly known places was marvellous, and there was not much of the unexpected or downright impossible that she couldn't cope with in the end. She and many of her contemporaries were the natural successors to those women, who in the previous century had travelled the Empire not seeing home for decades or longer, all the time supporting their husbands in some far flung corner of the world where British interests needed to be upheld. What lucky people were I and those like me who married such women.

1984-1986.

These years saw us able to again live in our own house and enjoy a degree of normality for a reasonable period. At the start of 1984 I was to attend a course at the Royal College of Defence Studies for a year. The RCDS or the Imperial Defence College as it was known until a name change took place in the 1970s to reflect the altered circumstances of Britain's relationship with the rest of the world, was housed in Belgrave Square in a fine Georgian House a few minutes' walk from Victoria. The college's role was to give its students the opportunity to broaden their outlook on the world and included learning about the machinery of government, international relationships, diplomacy, civilian government and politics with military management concentrated on tri-service working and strategic defence. It was also intended as a year when students were not put under undue pressure to give them time to develop their own thinking on such matters. About half the students were from the three British services being joined by some of our own diplomats, a couple of high ranking policemen and senior civil servants, and people of equivalent rank or status from countries like the US, NATO and the Commonwealth nations and one or two others, for example Israel and Japan.

It was a good year and I made or renewed many friendships. Nick Ansell, Bob Hodges, James Rucker, Francis Sugden all British Army; Chris Morgan and Charles Nickerson-Eckersley, nicknamed 'Back Axle' by his Naval friends, and Clive Evans and John Thomson from the RAF and many others were all good fun to be with. The pace was undemanding and we were given plenty of time to do our own thing. I used to travel from Hampshire to Waterloo taking a train at an hour more appropriate for the 'managing director' class of commuter than the more lowly office 'slogger', and then walked slowly over Westminster Bridge to Belgrave Square, savouring the sights and sounds of the West End.

By great coincidence the Commandant of the College was Michael Gow! It was the third time that I was to serve under him and, being the person he was and serving his last appointment in a long career, he was pretty relaxed adding to the enjoyment of the rest of us. His wife, Jane, added her bit too, being naturally rather fey and, maintaining she didn't understand the college or what it did, she always made a beeline for Rosa who came to see herself as Jane's unofficial ADC! Also at the college was another Scots Guardsman, Christopher Airy, who was the senior Army instructor.

Guardsmen at the RCDS in 1984.
John Baskervyle Glegg; DMN; Michael Gow; Christopher Airy and Michael Hicks.

Apart from lectures and seminars we went on a number of visits, mainly to industrial, civic or government institutions. I remember three fascinating days in East Anglia when we visited organisations as diverse as Norwich Cathedral, the early morning fish market in Lowestoft, the Norfolk police and the Perkins diesel engine factory in Peterborough. We were led on that occasion by the College Rear Admiral, Arthur Baxter, a rather unworldly figure who had been head of the Royal Navy education branch and who had a higher opinion of his intellectual and diplomatic skills than was probably warranted. As fate would have it I found myself with him again four months later – this time as his deputy tour leader – when a dozen of us undertook an official tour to the Middle East, visiting Cyprus, Israel, Egypt, Abu Dhabi and Jordan. Again, a fascinating experience and well worthwhile, since we met President Mubarak of Egypt and the Crown Prince of Jordan and a number of very sinister Israeli officers and officials. Arthur nearly caused a diplomatic upset when we were 'in audience' with the Crown Prince, who, after expounding his views as to how the interminable Middle East crisis might be resolved, produced a book which he told us he had just written on the subject and handed it to Arthur. The latter glanced at it and then said in a dismissive tone, "Bought it at the airport – just read it," and handed it back. On another occasion when he was clearly bored with the senior minister with whom we were meeting, Arthur brought discussion to an abrupt end by saying to our illustrious host, "You know what it is like; we have a programme and it is time we moved on to the next serial." Jaws dropped!

Visiting a refugee camp in Jordan.

1984 was a lovely year for me, mainly because we were living at home; I was not unduly stretched and the RCDS was fun and an interesting experience, surrounded as I was by a good group of like-minded people. In August we were told where our next postings were to be. For me it was again to be the MOD serving mainly in the Military Secretary's (MS) department at Stanmore near Watford but with an office in the Main Building in Whitehall. My job was to be the Deputy Military Secretary (A); there were two such brigadier level appointments each working under the MS himself with (A) responsible for the careers, postings and promotions of Army officers of the rank of Colonel to General and (B) looking after the same issues for Lieutenant Colonels and below. David Mostyn was the MS and my colleague (B) was Peter Graham, a former Gordon Highlander and someone I had known since we were fellow adjutants of our respective battalions in Kenya twenty years previously. To be appointed to be DMS (A) was a joy since it was a job I had always rather wanted.

Undoubtedly the best news was that we could continue to live in Hampshire with me commuting by train to London or driving around the M25 to reach Stanmore, a journey of an hour and a half depending upon traffic which was then not as dense as it is now.

Personnel management has for long been organised by the Army in its own way with, anyway until the end of the last millennium, little transparency or outside regulation. That is not to say that the business of managing people, their aspirations or their career paths was not carried out scrupulously fairly and with considerable attention being given to the interests of the individual, just that more modern methods of assessment, job advertising and appeal mechanisms had not until relatively recently been employed, basically because the necessary computer systems had not then been developed. The system broadly suited the circumstances of the time. It was a proven, workable mechanism and was clearly understood even if its decisions might not always have been welcome to those affected.

Through a system of grading, interviews, promotion and selection boards officers' preferences and aspirations were carefully analysed and recorded with capabilities and appointments being matched as closely as possible to serve the best interests of both the Army and the individual. What I really enjoyed about my job was the personal contact I had with individual officers to discuss their futures and to try to meet their wishes, as well as the needs of the service. Of course, there were times when we got it wrong and placed an individual in an unsuitable job but they were few and far between. Difficult to manage though were disappointed expectations; it is human nature that we should all believe that we are deserving of promotion to the next level and, being ambitious, resent a contemporary who achieves it when we don't. It was the judgement of senior officers who literally read hundreds of reports on an individual going back maybe twenty years or more, sitting on a board of six or so contemporaries debating the merits of an officer for promotion or a particular appointment. Decisions were fairly arrived at but, because the higher you go in any organisation the competition becomes more intense, there were inevitable casualties along the way. It is like that in all walks of life.

An MS Board in session. L to R: David Mostyn; DMN; Peter Woolley and members of the board (Messrs Keighley, Beckett, Evans, Watkins, Waters and Inge).

Managing bruised or damaged egos was one of my responsibilities and it was not always easy to explain to an aggrieved brigadier who thought he deserved to be promoted to two-star rank why he was not to be. When in London I tried to let those who needed to be told the unvarnished truth why it was so, face to face. However, it had to be done and I like to think I didn't lose too many friends in the process. One of my ploys was to take an individual out to lunch at Sheekys, a fish restaurant off Leicester Square to help to break 'bad news'.

I was well supported at Stanmore where the 'engine room' of the MS department was located, by a team of experienced officers: Peter Woolley and later Jonnie Hall were my deputies respectively and both worked tirelessly to get the system right to achieve the best for the individual officer, whilst satisfying the needs of the Army. One 'perk' of the system was that the two of them, Peter Graham or I would in turn visit the Army stationed overseas to talk to individual officers to learn preferences or personal requirements which could influence where they might next be sent. As a result, I visited such places as Hong Kong, Brunei, Zimbabwe and Gibraltar to discuss careers and postings, sadly unaccompanied by Rosa except to Zimbabwe when we were both able to stay with the Hodges and the Parsons, all of whom were at the time based with the British Military Training Assistance Team. It was a lovely visit to an idyllic country before it became irreparably embroiled in the politics of the Mugabe era.

Zimbabwe with Andrew and Romy Parsons.

Living at South Warnborough gave us some much-appreciated stability over the years I was working in the London area. Towards the end of 1986 Nicholas had left Cheltenham and had been accepted at York University to read history and politics. Hughie too was about to leave Cheltenham and had decided to apply to read law at Southampton before later going to law school at Guildford. However, Willie, four years behind Hughie, had just left Wellesley House and, after much thought, it was decided that his dyslexia could best be accommodated if he was to attend Grenville College near Bideford in Devon. This was not an easy decision but much as Rosa and I would have liked him to follow the other two to Cheltenham, it was clear that his best interests would be served by going to Grenville. It was undoubtedly the correct decision and both David Powell Price, the headmaster, and David Young, his house master, did him proud. He later went on to the Royal Agricultural College at Cirencester achieving a degree in land management.

Willie's Confirmation with his godparents Barney Cockcroft and Miranda Lindsay, their spouses and Rosa's mother at Bideford.

Two close family deaths sadly occurred in the same period. My mother died in March 1986 aged eighty-three, having moved to Warren Lodge, a residential home near Finchampstead from her home at Shellbrook near Ellesmere a year or so earlier; it was a sadly necessary move and bringing her south made it easier for Carolyn and I to visit her, although probably less so for Christopher. Ten months earlier Oliver Onions, sister Mary Anne's husband, had died in Dublin from a heart disease leaving two children, Mark and Roseanna. At the time, Oliver was farming outside Port Laois and Mary Anne continued to do so until Mark took over about ten years ago, continuing the family tradition.

2nd Infantry Division 1987-1989.

The Queen travelled to York for the re-dedication of the Minster's South Transept after the fire of 1984. She was received with a guard of Honour at York Railway Station in 1988. L to R: DMN; Marcus Worsley and Henry Woods. Willie Swinton, ADC, on the left.

Patrick Palmer, an Argyll, who had taken over from David Mostyn as MS, called me into his office one day in July 1987 to tell me I had been selected to take over command of 2nd Infantry Division based in York in November that year. This meant promotion to major general and a command which most of my contemporaries would have given anything for; I was indeed very fortunate. Charles Guthrie, a Welsh Guardsman was my predecessor.

The division, numbering around 18,000 all ranks, was spread across North East England from Northumberland to Lincolnshire and comprised both regular and Territorial Army units, the largest concentration being in the Catterick area of North Yorkshire, now the biggest military garrison in Europe. My headquarters was in Imphal Barracks in the Fulford Road on the south side of York and the GOC's house was opposite; Danesmead was originally a dental surgery but had been taken over by the Army in the 1970s. It was a comfortable and convenient place to live and gave considerable scope for entertaining local people, friends and the military hierarchy when they descended upon us. Meanwhile we had once again to let South Warnborough, this time to Jeremy and Sue Moger, whom we had known in Hohne and who were fortunately available since they were looking for somewhere to rent other than a military quarter. They looked after the house immaculately in our absence.

Danesmead.

Without going into great detail, the role of the Division was to reinforce British troops in Germany in a period known as 'transition to war'. This would have been the short time when it might become clear that the Soviet Union was about to launch an attack on Western Europe. Under the terms agreed by members of the NATO alliance at its inception that 'an attack on one member would be assumed to be an attack on all', the three British divisions already based in Western Germany and under the alliance's unified command, would deploy to pre-determined battle stations along with their NATO allies to counter the identified threat. At the same time the role of 2nd Division would be to move to Germany to reinforce their sister divisions, primarily by occupying positions to the rear of the main deployment areas.

Detailed plans were in place for deployment to the Continent and these were continually updated. It would have been a massive deployment utilising considerable sea and air resources, taking several days. In addition, the operational areas to be occupied on arrival were pre planned and had been made known to generations of commanders, who might one day need to occupy them. The unknown factor was of course that nobody could say what might be the circumstances under which the Division would deploy and the extent to which movement to the Continent might be disrupted by pre-emptive enemy action. I and my staff spent many hours in the Divisional War Room in York trying to second guess the problems we might face.

In addition to commanding 2nd Division with its mix of regular and territorial units, I also had command of other Army units which were based in North East England. The military district comprised the then eight counties of the north east from Berwick upon Tweed to Lincoln, the majority being home defence units with the operational role of maintaining security should Britain be threatened by an attack or invasion by an aggressor. Again in 'transition to war' when I and my staff would have deployed to Germany, my peacetime deputy, Brigadier Tony Wells and later Brigadier Dick Mundell, would take command of this force and conduct any necessary operations. Finally, there were a number of static units located in the district with peace time roles in training and logistics, all of which came under the central 2nd Division/ North East District peacetime command. It was a busy and most absorbing command and I greatly enjoyed my time in York.

I was well supported by my subordinates. Peter Woolley commanded 24th Airportable Brigade with Tim Bevan and Simon Firth commanding the two Territorial Army brigades in 2nd Division, based respectively at Topcliffe in North Yorkshire and at Chilwell near Nottingham. At divisional headquarters my chief of staff was Julian Browne, to be followed in due course by David Cranston with Malcolm Gilbertson responsible for the logistic and disciplinary side of life. They in their turn were sustained by a number of serving and retired officers working in Imphal Barracks. It was a cohesive and efficient team and supported me and the units under my command well. I spent much of my time visiting units and getting to know the principal personalities, something which I always enjoyed, although in the case of TA units, visits usually took place in the evenings when soldiers had finished their civilian employment and donned uniform before reporting to their drill hall for two or three hours training. As might be expected the TA comprised a wide mixture of people drawn from every background you could imagine.

Meanwhile I had external links to maintain to Army Headquarters near Salisbury as well as to the various civil authorities in whose administrative districts, military units were deployed; mayors, chief executives, MPs and others all appeared on the radar at some stage or another and of course there were lots of people across the district, but mainly in North Yorkshire, who were happy to associate themselves with the military. I had eight lord lieutenants in the command and they were important, not least because of their traditional links to the TA towards which they had certain statutory responsibilities. All were helpful and all made my job easier and more interesting.

Rosa and her mother.

This is not the place to record all those whom we met while living in York but it seemed there were an awful lot of them at the time! Rosa, Sergeant Taylor and Corporal Rutherford at Danesmead, and David Wilson and later Willie Swinton, my two ADCs, who did a year each, and Anne Barlow, my PA in the office, all helped with arranging life and entertaining and hosting people, which was all part of the boss's role. I can't think how many guests we entertained at Danesmead – often a mix of military visitors and civilian friends – during our two years, but both Rosa and I felt that, my having been given such an important and enjoyable job, it was for us to repay that trust and to do the job properly. I always felt that those living in my area of command expected 'their general' to take note and be well disposed to them in return for the support and friendship they gave us, and rightly so.

Our busy two years involved a lot of fun as well as hard work. Rosa took Cuckoo up to York and Eddy and Sarah York at Hutton Wandesley kindly provided a base where she could be stabled and from where Rosa could hunt, principally with the Middleton. I received a number of invitations to shoot locally and, after 1989, I kept on a gun at Dalton on the edge of the Lake District owned by Tony Mason Hornby, where brother Peter also had a gun and where he had previously persuaded me to join the syndicate. The drive across to Lancashire from Yorkshire is a lovely one and I always enjoyed Dalton. Nicholas was at the University for most of our time at Danesmead; initially I think he was a bit peeved that, having got away from us in Hampshire, he learnt that we were following him north to York! However early mild annoyance turned to satisfaction when he came to realise the advantages of the occasional decent meal and a responsive laundry service. I don't think we cramped his style nor indeed impinged upon his life at the University from where he graduated with a 2:1 degree in July 1989. It was good to have him and his friends call in from time to time to dilute the self-importance of some of our other visitors!

Nicholas graduated from York University in 1989.

Christopher and Penelope at Newby Hall near Ripon.

Visiting the Humber Bridge.

A visit to Sharlston Colliery near Wakefield with David Wilson.

All good things must come to an end and I handed over command of the division in November 1989 to Mike Rose, a Coldstreamer. By that time, we had decided to stay in Yorkshire and had bought a house near Malton into which we moved on leaving Danesmead, but more of that later. A little time before we left I had been told that my next job was to be in the MOD where I was to be appointed the Director General of the Territorial Army and Organisation, a two star director level position working directly to the CGS; there was a certain inevitability in my being chosen for such a job given my immediate past experience, but it was not the post I would necessarily have chosen for myself had I been given the option. However, I had been fortunate to have been given command of 2nd Division, one of the best four operational major general command appointments in the Army at that time, and so really had no reason to complain.

1990-1992.

Before we left York, guessing that I was next destined to be posted to do a job in London, Rosa and I decided that, should that be the case, rather than live there on a permanent basis, I should weekly commute from Yorkshire returning home at week-ends. We therefore purchased a flat in a house at 72. Tachbrook Street in Pimlico, not far from Victoria, and a twenty minute walk from the MOD. It was at the top of the building and made a good base in a relatively quiet street.

In parallel but a little before that purchase, we had decided that longer term our future probably lay in North Yorkshire, an area we had come to greatly enjoy having been widely welcomed when we arrived in York in 1987 and having made a host of good friends since. In addition, we loved the countryside and the blunt but genuine way that people in the North of England conducted their lives. I can think of few other rural counties, other than possibly Shropshire, Devon, Cumbria or Northumberland which exude the same feelings of well-being and enjoyment, coupled with down to earth attitudes. I had no wish to return to my family roots in Cheshire, by then anyway much diluted, and Rosa felt that a return to Gloucestershire, however much she had relished her formative years there, was not what she wished for. Overall it was not therefore a difficult decision and in late 1988 we asked Tim Blenkin, at the time working in the Jackson Stops York office, to find us a house expecting a long and rather fruitless search with little to show for it at the end.

What we wanted was a medium sized house in pleasant countryside, with stables and some outbuildings and suitable grazing for a horse or two, a manageable garden, easy access to York and the rail network, a pleasant village and friendly neighbours. Thanks to Tim's efforts and Rosa's timing in going to the Jackson Stops office at exactly the right moment, that is more or less what we got! Minster Hill, sixteen miles from York just to the west of Malton, was on the market for just under £400,000 and apart from one other bidder, there was seemingly not much competition. To cut a long story short we persevered with our bid and eventually got the house. We had fallen on our feet!

What sold us the notion that we wanted to live there? Basically, it fitted all our criteria and most importantly gave Rosa scope for two of her main interests: riding and gardening. For me it was in lovely countryside with magnificent views of the Yorkshire Wolds to the east, was easily accessible to the main A64 road to York, surely one of the most beautiful and interesting provincial cities in Britain, with the railway line from Scarborough to York passing a few hundred yards to the front, close enough to be there but not to intrude; for me, a lifelong railway fan, that was attractive. There is something about the passage of trains: they pass at allotted times and when they pass by on schedule, they reassure one's sub conscious that 'all is well with the world'. Anyway, that is how it has always seemed to me!

We gained possession of Minster Hill in the spring of 1989 but did not move in until later, once we had vacated Danesmead. There was quite a bit of work to be done and Peter Ingram and his team from Langton undertook alterations. It has proved an ideal house for us, not only because of its position and accessibility but the size was right, it had the outside buildings we wanted and the village of Huttons Ambo proved to be a welcoming and friendly community. If there was a downside it would be that getting onto the A64 can take time and nerve because the traffic is often relentless, especially in the holiday season when the population of the coastal area of the county probably trebles with visitors holidaying at the seaside; to make the point that the village is landlocked by the main road with no other way of escape, I often say 'we take our lives in our hands' when we try to leave Minster Hill; clearly something of an exaggeration and in the thirty years we have now been here no one has yet been killed or seriously hurt, although there have been some narrow escapes. Nonetheless as such statements go, there is more than a little truth in it.

My new job in London was important but, as so often with staff appointments involving tri-service working with government ministers and civil servants, it was not always very productive and inevitably frustrating. My responsibilities involved organisational and structural oversight of both the regular and the volunteer armies with a series of other supervisory roles in respect of the TA. In 1990 the services were about to be subjected to one of those periodic reviews so beloved of politicians searching for economies, under a programme titled 'Options for Change' which in the case of the Army broadly speaking involved measures to rationalise and reduce the number of regular units, while at the same time placing more emphasis on the roles to be played by reserve forces. As can be imagined it gave rise to great anxiety in certain quarters, involved much lobbying and not a little unhappiness when final outcomes became known. I spent many hours with my boss, General John Chapple, the CGS, and his immediate deputy, Richard Swinburn, debating the many options under consideration which had eventually to be decided by the Army Board. As might be expected Colonels of Regiments, Lord Lieutenants and even Royalty all lobbied in an attempt to deflect or destroy a particular option considered, anyway by them, to be untenable or locally unacceptable.

In due course, proposals became firm plans, resulting in a number of regular Army regiments of all arms and services being reduced or amalgamated. At the same time some TA units were similarly affected although overall numbers increased in the expectation that their future contribution to defence would expand. The eventual results were probably the best to be achieved given the pressures on the defence budget at that time but were not welcome in that many regimental officers considered they had been let down by their superiors, especially when further reviews were ordered in the mid-1990s. In addition, the First Gulf War took place in 1991 and many wondered how we could undertake a major reduction in force levels when we were about to fight what could be a major campaign in the Middle East.

More in depth analysis of Options for Change would be tedious; suffice it to say it happened, the world didn't stop and the services rose to the challenge of becoming leaner and no doubt more capable in a number of ways. However, it was sad to see the disillusionment felt by many people at the time and to later learn that some of the operational benefits forecast for the TA in particular, have not been realised.

Working for John Chapple was quite a revelation. He had served much of his career with the Gurkhas and was a consummate staff officer, clear minded and logical in his assessment of what should be the eventual outcome of the reorganisation foist upon him as professional head of the Army by ministers. However, he was not a great communicator – nicknamed the 'Buddha' by some on account of his inscrutable attitude – and his inscrutability often made his thought processes difficult to read. I am not sure that I always read him correctly and that may well have coloured his opinion of me.

There were of course moments of relief from the MOD grind, principally due to my responsibilities to the TA and the Army cadets. I travelled a fair amount to visit units and to talk to gatherings of officers to brief them about the impending changes and hopefully to still some of the criticisms as to how the process of change was being handled at the top. I was not always successful but at least I and my staff made a determined effort to keep people informed, if not necessarily on side as a result of what they heard. So many of the problems in the world today stem from a lack of communication, a situation easily rectified if leaders have the courage to tell the truth.

Early in 1992, John Chapple made it known to me that there would be no further job for me once my present tenure came to an end. I was therefore to leave the Army that April aged fifty-four after thirty-six years serving Queen and Country. I had harboured the hope that I might be promoted to three-star rank and be selected for another appointment, but it was not to be. As might be expected I was very disappointed because I knew within myself that I had both the service experience and personal energy to continue contributing. Some, I suspect, thought it was poetic justice after all those occasions when I had had to 'read the tea leaves' to officers when they came to seek advice when I was working for the Military Secretary six years previously, culminating in my advising them that their future in the Army was unfortunately limited! The brutal truth is that the pyramid to be climbed to reach the top of any organisation gets steeper the higher you go and only the very ablest (or the luckiest!) reach the summit. The tragedy is that, as a result, much still useable talent is wasted but that never seems to be acknowledged. Maybe I was lucky to have managed to get as far as I did.

My MOD staff gave me a lovely farewell lunch – ironically at Sheekys in St Martin's Lane – after which I left the office for the last time. At the time it seemed rather a sad way to end thirty-six years of service – in particular the happy and fruitful times spent with my fellow Scots Guardsmen – and I recall feeling rather empty as I caught the 5pm train from King's Cross back to York and Minster Hill on my final journey home. It was not the way I would have chosen to end a lifetime spent in a single profession but there was little to be done about that and indeed a new world soon started to emerge.

Minster Hill.

Chapter Five

Minster Hill and life in North Yorkshire.

W hat was I going to do, retired from my main career at the comparatively early age of fifty-four? Too old to be of much interest to a future employer but too young not to undertake some useful occupation. This is a dilemma faced by generations of service officers – and increasingly by many people from other walks of life who find themselves retiring early in today's world – who, unless they are destined for the very top of their service, must retire at fifty-five and seek a second career job which is both satisfying and right for them. There is also the not irrelevant issue of how otherwise the bills will be paid. A pension, although not ungenerous, makes only limited provision. However, the armed services have always had a policy of retiring people at the age of fifty-five, which is logical in view of the physical demands of the profession, if not the wish of an individual to continue making a worthwhile contribution to society in that particular field.

Rosa and I had already agreed that I would not look for anything in London; separation and long distance weekly commuting were not what either of us wanted and, having done it for two years while in the MOD, I did not wish to continue such a life; better therefore to capitalise on our decision to remain in Yorkshire where we had bought a suitable house. In my last year or so in the Army determined efforts had been made by the MOD – in particular by the then Adjutant General, David Ramsbotham, a very energetic former Green Jacket officer – to persuade employers in the business and commercial worlds that former Army officers had much to offer in terms of intelligence, energy and adaptability and that most would turn their hands to whatever might be asked of them. As a result, in my last year I had visited an employment agency and was put on their books as a possible candidate for something. Sadly, nothing came of that initiative.

One area which did interest me was to do something in politics. Having had a father in law who had been an MP and, having myself always possessed an interest in how political management worked, I put my name forward to be a Conservative candidate and was accepted by Party Headquarters. I think it was more the representational side that really attracted me – the idea of being the person to promote and protect the interests of constituents – more than the thought of being in a position to decide the Nation's future in Parliament. However, it was not to happen and while I reached the final shortlist for selection for four or five constituency Conservative Associations, including being the runner up at Berwick on Tweed, I never made it to become the final candidate. Maybe that was because I was considered to be too old or from the wrong background: who knows? However, I did get a chance to go into politics when five years later I was elected to serve as a councillor on the North Yorkshire County Council and did so for eight years. In retrospect my rejection for a parliamentary seat may have been a fortuitous escape; the conduct of politics and the lives of the current generation of practitioners have both changed so markedly over the last two decades as to cause the House of Commons to become a different, less respected and less absorbing place than it was. Judging by how the 650 MPs who sit in parliament today are allegedly viewed by their constituents, how they are continually harried by the media and in some instances castigated on social media, often unjustly, it is all too easy to see why good and capable people don't enter the political arena today.

I soon started to put out feelers locally and was one day asked by the Chairman of the Yorkshire Regional Health Authority if I would consider taking the chairmanship of the North Yorkshire Ambulance Service, a recently formed health trust under the Conservative Government's NHS reforms which had been put in place gradually over the last two decades of the century. It was likely to be an important assignment with many challenges and I accepted. The work involved close contact with people, providing leadership, representing the trust in the wider health environment and chairing a board of non-executive directors which included Michael Oakley and Angela Widdowes, both of whom we had come to know well since we first arrived in York. Mike King, an experienced and energetic, if rather an abrasive ambulanceman, was the CEO. It was interesting and at times daunting working alongside a highly trained and proficient team of medical specialists, learning of the stresses encountered in their professional lives and acquainting myself with some of the issues with which the service was confronted on an almost daily basis; response times, types of ambulances, the required professional skills, to say nothing of the emotional and physical pressures under which staff had to operate when dealing with life threatening issues. It always amazed me that the general public could even think about harassing those in the emergency services attending an incident; whether it was because they saw ambulancemen, firemen and police officers as representatives of authority and therefore legitimate targets for abuse or worse, or, because they saw ambulances in particular, when they had momentarily to be left unattended in order to concentrate on a patient, as a likely place to find drugs, I never knew. The staff were high grade, dedicated and highly qualified medical professionals with a strong sense of duty but not always easy to deal with, the pressures under which they often had to work making for an understandable venting of feelings. When I eventually left I took with me memories of a very committed and humane group of people.

Needless to say, money to run the service was a perennial problem. The NHS reforms were originally intended to give individual units the autonomy to manage themselves and to cut out waste and bureaucracy, all of which were laudable objectives but, in the endless scramble to acquire a reasonable level of resourcing, relationships within the NHS tended to fray and unwelcome solutions were imposed from above, thereby devaluing the original ethos of the trust system. I always suspected that those civil servants tasked with implementing the new system of health care, devised by politicians and then passed to them for implementation, were never sold on the system and probably determined from the start to undermine it and to wrest back the influence they had lost. Eventually the Yorkshire Region was amalgamated with its sister organisation based in Newcastle with most of the top appointments going to people from there. A more authoritarian approach soon emerged.

I did five and a half years as Chairman and towards the end the trust was faced by problems of poor management and alleged bullying, which were unfortunately compounded by a failure in the service control room to get an emergency ambulance to an incident, as a result of which a young boy died. It was an avoidable mistake and we paid dearly for it with a public enquiry and much critical comment in the media, including a Channel 4 Dispatches programme investigating our mistakes. Mike King had to go and was dismissed by the Board and, in the face of unrelenting media pressure and personal criticism of me as Chairman, I decided that it would be best for me to step down in order to allow the Trust to recover its equilibrium. In May 1977, I therefore tendered my resignation, disappointed at the turn of events but satisfied that much had been achieved under my leadership. In due course NYAS was amalgamated with three other ambulance trusts to form the Yorkshire Ambulance Service, something which should probably have been done from the outset had politicians and civil servants had the courage and vision to put their full weight behind their own original conceptual plans.

Was I unwise to get involved in the first place? I don't think so and as already said I think much was achieved; most importantly the establishment of mutual respect in the service between management and staff which had been developed early on, although problems towards the end of my time clearly set things back. For me it was a case of learning by experience. Judging by events since 1997 the NHS and its component trusts continue to be regarded by politicians, the media and the public as easy targets, to be criticised and derided at will, usually without the critics knowing the real circumstances of most issues. As so often in life the best intended plans can be destroyed or diminished by ignorant human reaction. Many people who had achieved much in their previous lives before stepping forward to undertake responsibilities in helping to run NHS trusts, were later badly let down by politicians and civil servants who gave them little or no preparation for their roles and then abandoned them when things didn't always go quite right.

In 1993, I stood for election to be the councillor for the Rillington division of the North Yorkshire County Council. The division covered a large rural area east of Malton encompassing the southern side of the North Yorks Moors, much of the Vale of Pickering and the northern slopes of the Yorkshire Wolds. It contained a number of quite large villages like Thornton le Dale, Rillington, Sherburn and Staxton and within its boundaries included the RAF Early Warning Station at Fylingdales with its 'golf ball' detection systems located high on the North Yorkshire Moors. An area of lovely countryside and about 5,000 constituents. However, on that occasion I was defeated by the sitting councillor – Ford Longman, a Liberal Democrat, – by just four votes. In May 1997 I tried again and, as I promised Ford I would, I beat him by a sizeable majority. I served for eight years in total standing down in 2005, serving my last three years as the deputy leader of the ruling Conservative group. It was interesting work involving the administration of education, social services and the highway network of England's largest county although there were other responsibilities, for instance licencing, trading standards and the planning of major industrial development. I thoroughly enjoyed the 'constituency' work and involved myself with the twenty-five or so villages in my area, visiting them to ensure that people knew who I was and how I could help them. Meetings, most of which were held in an evening to ensure that working councillors could get to them, could be tedious but were important because they revealed the concerns and aspirations of individual communities. When I left I received a number of letters thanking me for my help, a gesture which for me made it all worthwhile.

Life at County Hall in Northallerton was very different. I was a backbencher for my first three years but was then invited by David Ashton, the Conservative Group Leader, to join the Executive (known in some authorities as the Cabinet since local government reform in the late 1990s) and was made responsible initially for the Council's corporate affairs portfolio which included a host of minor tasks, and later Social Services where I worked closely with Rosemary Archer, the Director and her team. The latter were a knowledgeable and compassionate group of professionals and served the county well although their work was seldom recognised outside the Council. Rosemary was a very sensible and understanding director who sadly left in 2003 to take a similar role in Leeds. I cannot pretend that I was a natural to be the political 'lead' for social services and I found visits to residential homes, day care centres and private sector providers often palled, but there was a strong compassionate thread running through the work the directorate did which gave everyone involved a high degree of motivation. I often asked social workers what it was that attracted them to their work with the invariable reply that "they wouldn't wish to do anything else since they just loved the job". When one works 'on the inside' one usually sees the true worth of people and when I left it was with a feeling of great respect and no little thanks for those alongside whom

I had been privileged to serve. I was glad to have experienced how people, often derided by the public for their role in helping others, went about their tasks demonstrating compassion and indeed affection for those for whom they cared or who needed help.

There were aspects of life in County Hall which were not much fun. NYCC had generally good officers and in my time they were led by two high grade Chief Executives: John Ransford and Jeremy Walker, both of whom certainly knew their stuff. I never enjoyed meetings of the full Council which luckily only happened three times a year; they were occasions when political posturing could take place and some members would grandstand in order to make an abstruse point in order to win attention for a special, often irrelevant, issue. I think such occasions were disliked by most members. I eventually decided not to seek re-election in 2005 mainly because I felt that the Council 'agenda' was beginning to repeat itself with the same issues coming up again and again. In addition, I was finding that the fifty-minute journey from home to Northallerton was proving increasingly tedious, especially since I was becoming rather arthritic when sitting for a long time in the car. Despite that it had been a good eight years and I enjoyed it and the many people I encountered. I have invariably enjoyed canvassing at election time; when seeking election or re-election to NYCC Rosa always supported me and made a great fist of persuading people to vote for me. I often found that she could persuade an undecided voter by finding a subject of mutual interest like their garden or maybe their dog, thereby turning the conversation in that direction and winning their support! One learnt a lot when knocking on doors; for example, 1030am on a Saturday morning seemed to be the time when most people in Rillington took a bath! However, if people didn't wish to talk to you there were plenty of ways to put a canvasser off; meal times, watching TV, putting the children to bed, on the telephone or just plain they didn't like your politics, finally slamming the door in your face. However, people were generally good natured and usually more interested than they might wish to show and we never had many doors shut on us. My greatest supporter though was Shelia Clayton who lived at Ebberston and acted as my agent at election time. Forceful, fun and energetic she was a never ending source of local knowledge and great common sense, not surprising really as she was originally from Liverpool!

Both during and after my involvement with the Ambulance Service and later the County Council I accepted other tasks of a voluntary nature. One was membership of various local committees like the Transport Users' Consultative Committee, a Yorkshire pressure group designed to give the public an influence over local transport provision. If I remember the committee spent a lot of time hearing appeals against British Railways' plans to close little used stations; Church Fenton south of York was one but I can't remember what decision we arrived at, if any! When I first settled in Yorkshire I had an approach from Desmond Langley, my brigadier in Munster in 1976, who was Governor of the Church Lads and Church Girls Brigade, a Church of England youth organisation established in the last century. He asked me to become a trustee of the Brigade whose headquarters was based in the Dearne valley near Rotherham, which I did. The brigade was organised on quasi-military lines, was based principally but not exclusively in the North of England and did excellent work to help and guide young people.

I also did two stints as chairman of the Ryedale Constituency Conservative Association and later its successor organisation when the constituency boundaries were redrawn joining Thirsk and Malton together. I had been involved with the local Conservatives ever since we came to live at Huttons Ambo. Serving as an officer in a local political organisation is a commitment increasingly avoided by able people, who can quickly become frustrated by the way in which our party political systems operate. In my view Conservative Central Office have never really understood how to treat local party organisations, tending to view them at best with suspicion, at worst with a mixture of disdain or indifference. I suspect this arises because CCO staff, like a number of MPs of all parties, tend to lose touch with reality when they arrive in the 'Westminster environment' forgetting those, in the case of MPs, who sent them there in the first place.

Over several years of active involvement, I and the local committee – and indeed my successors as chairman – had to deal with a variety of issues most of which arose because of an individual's reaction to a policy advocated by the Party. John Greenway represented the constituency for most of my time to be followed in 2005 by Anne McIntosh and a few years later by Kevin Hollinrake. Anne was an enigma; capable, energetic and effective but secretive and disinclined to work closely with those whose voluntary role it was to provide support for her at constituency level; she was not a team player and paid the price for an increasingly unreasonable attitude which eventually led to her deselection which was accompanied by the inevitable political histrionics, both locally and at Westminster. Her successor, Kevin Hollinrake, is proving himself to be a steady and approachable MP using his experience as a businessman combined with a sure and welcoming touch. He is seemingly effective in Parliament and deals sensibly with local issues. The most contentious of these at the moment is the intention to drill deep into the earth in order to conduct the hydraulic fracturing of hydrocarbon mineral reserves of oil and gas deep beneath the Vale of Pickering, using techniques involving hydraulics, chemicals and water; intense feelings about 'fracking' have manifested themselves on both sides of the argument and the lobby against extraction plans has now established a temporary camp in the constituency as part of their protest, aimed at frustrating operations. Kevin has played a straight bat taking a middle course and advocating patience to allow reasoned analysis of the outcome if or when fracking actually takes place, while acquainting himself with all sides of the argument.

At the time of writing this book in 2018 a number of landowners in Ryedale, including here at Minster Hill, have been approached to allow geo-physical surveys on their land to identify mineral reserves and possible means of extracting oil and gas should that be deemed expedient and economical. Inevitably there are arguments on both sides and it is clear that a vocal opposition is opposed to any form of fracking on environmental and safety grounds. However, there are others who can see the potential that fracking gives for Britain's self-sustainability in the field of energy provision, who believe that, as a nation, we should embrace measures that allow us to become less dependent on countries like Russia and Saudi Arabia for future supplies. There is a certain inevitability in all of this and I believe that fracking will eventually happen; after all a Government which knows it is sitting on very large reserves of oil and gas which might provide the nation with energy for fifty years or more would be criminally irresponsible if it did not seek to discover the scale of those resources and the ease with which they might be extracted. We shall see what happens but we have said we will permit surveys on the small amount of land we have at Minster Hill. However, I suspect the issue of fracking will outlive me.

Other non 'political' commitments also came my way. Early on after retirement

I was invited by Teddy Denison, the Vice Chairman of the Governing Body and Robin Pittman, the sitting Headmaster, to become a governor of St Peter's School in York. The school is the second oldest in Britain having been founded in 627AD and today provides fee paying education for children from the age of eight to eighteen on a co-educational basis, with a number of pupils boarding. The campus with several acres of playing fields, is situated in Clifton. When I became involved there were up to nineteen governors, representing a variety of interests and, until 1995 the governing body was always chaired by the Dean of York, then John Southgate, with some governors being nominated by outside bodies while others were co-opted. The school was generally very successful in achieving high standards, Robin Pittman and his two successors in my time – Andrew Trotman and Richard Smyth – each proving to be able, humane and firm headmasters and the school today continues in similar fashion under Leo Winkley.

The Governors of St Peter's School, 2005. As fine a group as I could have hoped for.

It was a privilege to sit on the governing body and to be involved in furthering the aspirations and plans to permit the expansion of the school's facilities.

Teddy took over as Chairman in 1995 and five years later I followed him, a great honour since I had no local connections nor was I a former pupil. The role of chairman of a school like St Peter's can be a deeply satisfying and during my tenure we had the additional challenge of expanding the campus. Co-terminus on our western boundary was a state school – Queen Anne's – which York City Council had recently declared to be surplus to their requirements and had therefore been put up for sale. The site was ideal for use as an educational facility or for housing and competition was expected to be keen, especially from some of the other private schools in the area, who were clearly as determined as St Peter's to acquire it. One competitor was Bootham, a Quaker school and similar in role to St Peter's which, had they managed to purchase the site, could have made life very awkward because of the resulting close proximity of the two establishments. There were other complications including affordability, the views of local residents and a concern that the City Council, Labour controlled at the time, might not be minded to sell a publicly owned asset to a private school. We had some tense moments during negotiations which were handled by two York based governors, Nicholas Shepherd and Richard Wood, both of whom were Old Peterites and had very considerable experience of the York property market and the workings of the council. Between them they handled negotiations with skill and common sense and eventually the decision was made to sell Queen Anne's to St Peter's. As a result, the site and its fine buildings were used to house our junior school – St Olave's – while the senior school was able to undertake a much-needed expansion into the areas vacated. It was an excellent outcome and in retrospect it is hard to contemplate what life might have been like if the decision had gone another way.

I served five years as Chairman and handed over to John Pike, a Leeds solicitor, in 2005. My fourteen years as a governor had given me real gratification and a deep insight into how a public school must operate, often under the hostile gaze of the outside world. Being headmaster of such an establishment was no easy task and the need to balance so many competing interests was at times unenviable; pupils, parents, staff, the governing body, former pupils and the local community could all bring their own problems which had to be juggled in the interests of the wider school. My role as chairman was to support the headmaster or, when necessary, to offer unambiguous advice if I thought he was wrong. That the latter never occurred says much for the way the two incumbents I served alongside – Andrew Trotman and Richard Smyth – handled their difficult task. Overall, I look back with pleasure on the friendships I made over fourteen years with both staff and governors and shall always be grateful for the opportunity to have been involved with St Peter's.

As might have been expected, leaving the Army meant a clean break with what had been my sole occupation up until that time; professions such as that of a solicitor, accountant or clergyman customarily have a tendency to retain their senior people as consultants on retirement in order to further harness their experience and knowledge, often in return for an honorarium, a system that benefits both parties and allows those retiring to remain involved but to reduce their workload. Not so other professions, including the Army, where retirement means just that. However, in the case of the regiment it was slightly different; when I had joined the Scots Guards in 1956 I became part of a family and thirty-six years later I was still part of that family enjoying the embrace of my fellow guardsmen and memories of experiences once shared. This meant being involved to a lesser extent, but on occasions being useful.

Soon after I retired, Kim Ross, commanding the regiment at the time, asked me if I would bring the history of the Scots Guards up to date, something I was only too happy to do and for a number of reasons: first I enjoy writing, while the period he had in mind were the years 1956, the year when the last history had concluded, to 1993, a period which coincided almost exactly with my own time in the Army. In addition, such a task would allow me to stay in touch with people whom I knew well and respected and with whom I was reluctant to lose touch. In a way I suppose it was the equivalent of being a consultant for a period. For almost two years I researched the regiment's history and records at RHQ in Wellington Barracks, interviewed past leaders such as commanding officers and RSMs, travelled around the country to meet them and others, even going down to the Falkland Islands to view the 1982 Battle of Tumbledown where the 2nd Battalion under M.I.E Scott had so distinguished itself in the campaign to retake the islands after the Argentine invasion that summer. An added bonus was that ten years after the battle, Iain Mackay-Dick who had been Mike's second in command in 1982, was by then commanding the Falklands Garrison. Together we toured the battlefield drawing upon his unique knowledge of the events of June 1982 to bring alive the battalion's hard-fought engagement with their Argentine adversaries at

Tumbledown, a victory which led to the latter's eventual surrender.

My research and the writing up of each commanding officer's period in command proceeded in parallel and, once completed, I sent the officer concerned a draft to ensure that he agreed the accuracy and fairness of what I had written. As far as I recall no one challenged those drafts other than to suggest a degree of emphasis, a date or a name which pleased me since not to have shown important personalities a draft could have led to arguments post publication resulting in the final book being devalued. Compiling the factual annexes which were a vital part of such an historical record, was time consuming but vital if the book was to be trusted as a reference work containing essential regimental records. In this task I was assisted by Peter Le Marchand whose meticulous work greatly helped the overall project.

Among Friends. The Scots Guards 1956-1993 was published in June 1995 by Leo Cooper in London. It ran to nearly 300 pages and was generally well received within regimental circles. Oliver Lindsay, the Editor of the *Guards Magazine* and himself a consummate historian, in reviewing the book that summer, wrote that "It is very much a family history. Indeed, one of the aims Murray Naylor set himself was to produce a history with which all Scots Guardsmen could identify, be they General or Guardsman". His comments reassured me as to the value of the work and subsequent reports confirmed that the book was indeed successful in meeting the challenge of inclusivity. Overall the project gave me immense satisfaction and provided a most suitable bridge in my transition from a career spent entirely as a soldier to life as a civilian.

Three years prior to the publication of *Among Friends* a tragic incident took place when the 1st Battalion of the regiment was serving in Belfast. Two guardsmen who were part of a patrol in the New Lodge district of the city were involved in a shooting incident when a man acting suspiciously, was shot and later died. The guardsmen concerned were later charged with murder, tried, convicted and sentenced to a term of imprisonment. The incident neatly illustrated the difficulties faced by soldiers serving on the streets of Northern Ireland who must at all times seek to protect the innocent and interfere as little as possible with everyday life, but at the same time must pursue those intent upon promoting terrorism and the destruction of the established order yet must do so within the law of the land. The regiment later established a 'release group' to attempt to give publicity to the two guardsmen's case and to persuade political leaders that their cases should be reviewed and they released. This followed a not dissimilar case brought by another regiment which had been successful. Along with Kim Ross, Michael Nurton, Ronnie Wilkie, Tony Heybourn and Sir David Scott-Barrett, I was a member of the release group which worked to present the guardsmen's case, in the process appointing Mark Haslam, a highly regarded lawyer, to develop an initiative through the courts while ourselves approaching several of the key political personalities in order to lobby for the two soldiers. The two men were later released as part of an amnesty when a number of convicted terrorists were also released but sadly the trial verdict of murder was never expunged. We worked hard to make our case for the two soldiers and undoubtedly succeeded in bringing their plight to public notice but overall achieved little, mainly because the politics surrounding any possibility of release tended to trump any considerations of even handedness when it came to reviewing the circumstances of the original incident. Personally, I found myself embroiled with a way of doing business which I found frustrating, often deceitful and at times thoroughly distasteful. Maybe we were naïve in thinking we could change the minds of those who had the power to act on behalf of the two soldiers.

A Scots Guards Association Dinner in Liverpool. Keith Reid on the right.

All regiments have associations which link serving members with those retired and the Scots Guards are no different. Because of my long family connections with Liverpool I was assigned to be a member of the Merseyside Branch soon after joining the regiment and in 1978, while still serving, became the Branch President taking over from Tim Mostyn. It was a great privilege and I subsequently served for twenty-five years, handing over to Niall Crichton-Stuart in 2003. I made some good friends but, since I was still serving for most of my tenure, was not always as available as the branch might have wished. Nonetheless we worked well together and in Keith Reid and Jimmy Horne I had two stalwart officers who shouldered most of the management duties, while prior to them Bill Silcock and Ron McHenry did similar excellent work. Sadly regimental associations in many parts of the Army have been in decline for a number of years now: younger soldiers are less interested in such organisations preferring a different form of socialising when they retire: the bonds generated when soldiers come together in battle are less pronounced after nearly seventy years of peace, although some post war deployments such as Kenya, Malaysia or the Falklands campaign still draw people to each other; also today's recruiting areas and modern practices have led to branches being mal-located from areas where the regiment's potential recruits now live. In Liverpool we experienced all these trends and, unless the branch and indeed several others elsewhere in the country, can arrest the decline in interest and involvement, they will not survive.

The Commonwealth War Graves Commission memorial to 2nd Division at Kohima and the famous tennis court.

The Kohima Educational Trust was another activity which kept me in close touch with the Army after I had retired. In recent years the Battle of Kohima, almost seventy-five years ago in 1944 when the 2nd British Division defeated a major Japanese thrust aimed at invading Eastern India, has been commemorated every July in York and still is. Possibly the hardest fought battle of the Second World War, over a period of six weeks the two sides slogged it out in the jungle covered hills around what was then the small town of Kohima, engaging each other in close quarter combat. The conditions were appalling: monsoonal rain, mud everywhere, near vertical hillsides, long periods of low mist rendering support from the air almost impossible and the difficulty of evacuating casualties, made it a battle more reminiscent of the First World War than the Second. To remember this epic engagement the remaining veterans, their families and others gather each year at the Kohima Memorial in the grounds of York Minster to commemorate those who died. It is now one of the few occasions associated with the last war when such a gathering still takes place.

March past to commemorate Kohima at York Minster 2004. (L to R): Generals Rose, Horsefield, Lord Slim, DMN, FMs Guthrie and Inge.

Over the years the number of those who actually fought at Kohima has inevitably declined although other ways of keeping alive memories have evolved. One, the brain child of the late Gordon Graham, himself a Cameron Highlander who fought at Kohima, was a proposal that an educational trust should be established, primarily to cement the links between the people of Nagaland of which Kohima is the State Capital, and Britain, as a token of esteem and gratitude for the contribution made by the Naga people to the defeat of the Japanese. It was therefore decided a programme of practical support, financed by the trust, was to be devised to supplement the Indian Government's educational provision for Naga school children. The trust was established in 2003 and has today raised a large amount of money leading, for instance, to the creation of scholarships, the provision of teaching materials, library books and support to children who can now stay overnight at school rather than as previously having to trek each day through jungle country. There is also a programme designed to permit individual teachers to hone their teaching skills.

Gordon Graham, who died aged ninety-four in 2014, provided the vision and energy to create this unique form of support to a people far removed from Britain who, in the normal course of events, could not have expected such generous help. His daughter, Sylvia May, is now the Chief Executive of the trust which operates in the UK to raise funds while the responsibility for advising and implementing the use of those funds is in the hands of the Kohima Educational Service, its sister organisation in Nagaland. It is a system which works tolerably well although over 6,000 miles communication can sometimes impede progress. I was the first chairman of the UK trustees and in 2016 had the honour of being appointed President in succession to Gordon. At the time of writing this short history the trust is about to celebrate the seventy-fifth anniversary of the battle in 2019.

The Church of England is another institution which seems to have absorbed much of my time over the last few years. Rosa and I are, and always have been, regular attenders at church, having been brought up in the Christian faith. It matters not to me that others may not share my religious beliefs although it saddens me that many people, while not actively participating or supporting their local church, demand that it remains open and available to them when needed but are not prepared to do anything to assist its survival. In a very real sense we seem to have become a society which only sees religion in terms of 'social' worship like baptisms, weddings and funerals or special feast days like Christmas. It is a sad reflection on today's society whose faith, if it exists at all, seems to spring not from a belief in God and the teachings of the Bible but from more materialistic creeds or pursuits. It must be very demoralising for those called by the Church to minister to their fellow men in today's increasingly agnostic world.

Over the nearly thirty years we have lived in Huttons Ambo Rosa and I have tried to support our local church of St Margaret of Scotland. Rosa was for a time secretary to the Parochial Church Council while I was a churchwarden for eight years. Today the church still manages to hold services, normally taken by the rector who is also the incumbent for another four parishes in the benefice, supplemented as necessary by retired clergy – including the inestimable Canon Bob Rogers – or lay members of the congregation; however, numbers have dwindled and sadly fund raising hardly exists. It is a sad reality that Huttons Ambo village hall attracts more interest and support than St Margaret's which is clearly seen as an anachronism by many. We have known five incumbents – all shared with neighbouring parishes – over the thirty or so years we have lived in the village: Peter Gregory; Ted Chapman; Chris Ellis; Chris Parkin and 'Taff' Morgan, the latter about to retire in 2018. None have stayed as long as their predecessors of forty or fifty years ago and it is not difficult to see why. The job of an incumbent has changed immeasurably: more communities to serve; more church bureaucracy to deal with; a general inclination on the part of many congregations to contribute less or indeed nothing to the promotion and maintenance of their church and its activities; a growing trend for incumbents to be disinclined to embrace pastoral work such as visiting, while many no doubt harbour the feeling that they are fighting an uphill battle to persuade people to support the Christian faith and take part in worship. I would have to admit to a great degree of sympathy with any incumbent who expressed such sentiments.

St Margaret's Church, Huttons Ambo. Visit by Archbishop Sentamu 2006.

I volunteered to stand for election to our local Deanery synod and later the York Diocesan synod once I stopped serving as a churchwarden. I later agreed to take over the role of lay chairman of the Southern Ryedale Deanery from Peter Hollier who had served for some years and was not in good health. I felt it was important to be involved in both bodies in order to know what was happening in the diocese and the church more widely. An account of the workings of either synod has no place in this personal history other than for me to say that I found both forums very frustrating, since little business of any real importance was ever transacted and the views and opinions of the laity seemed to count for very little. The same was true of meetings held by our suffragan bishop with his lay chairmen: we talked around issues but never reached firm conclusions since to do so was seen as the prerogative of the clergy, not the laity. I felt particularly disillusioned that neither the bishop nor either of the rural deans I served alongside apparently had any wish to involve me in real issues or their resolution. Probably my fault because of a tendency to speak my mind, but I firmly believe that until the hierarchy of the church is prepared to listen to and take real account of the views of lay people, harness their abilities and share decisions, little will change in the way church business is conducted. After all it is lay people who provide most of the resources to allow the church to exist. I hate to say it but the leadership given by senior clergy in the York Diocese over the last twenty years has been very ineffectual, with little sustained effort or encouragement to tackle the related issues of spiritual direction, the decline of the rural church and the inadequacy of financial support to provide for the future. A policy of 'no church closures' may sound good but in the long run it can only lead to further decline. What organisations across Britain have not in recent years been forced to change working practices, slim down their estate or rationalise their employment structures to survive? Not to have done so at a time when change might have been easier to justify, smacks of a refusal to face facts or to possess the courage to make unpopular decisions. As one whose life has been greatly influenced by the Church of England I am deeply saddened.

However, my dealings with York Diocese have not all been gloom or disappointment! In late 2008 I became a volunteer guide at York Minster, the idea of undertaking such a role having been suggested to me by Peter Lyddon, a former Greenjacket officer and at the time the recently retired Chapter Steward at the Minster. It was a suggestion I embraced with alacrity because it provided the challenge of discovering all about a remarkable medieval building, its history and purpose while allowing me to meet and talk with a wide range of people from all backgrounds when relating stories of such a very special place. I began with a weekly duty in early 2009 and gradually expanded that initial involvement by conducting special booked group tours and then later, hidden tours to those areas of the building not open to the public, like the Chapter House roof, the West End bell chambers and the Great West Window.

Nearly ten years on, I am beginning to find that my regular weekly tours are starting to pall, possibly because I have been doing them for too long and my descriptions and explanations are becoming rather unimaginative. As a result, I have cut back those tours concentrating instead on the less frequent group and hidden tours. Looking back over nine years I can only say how much pleasure and interest guiding at the Minster has given me, both in terms of meeting visitors and being part of a team, which includes those who really keep the place running like the vergers, the hosts and the Minster police, to say nothing of literally hundreds of volunteers, all in such wonderful, awe inspiring surroundings. To be truthful I hardly ever leave the Minster without feeling spiritually uplifted for having been inside its portals. That is something I would be hard pressed to say about many other great buildings.

A reader might think that after all our years in the Army we had done enough travelling by the time I retired but not so! After1992 we determined to see parts of the world where service to the Queen might not previously have taken me. Over a period of the next fifteen to twenty years Rosa and I flew around the globe twice to New Zealand, twice to South America, travelled across Canada and then sailed up the 'inside passage' to Alaska, earlier twice going to South Africa and later to Jordan, Vietnam, Mauritius, New England in the 'fall' and more recently to Europe. We stayed with relations and friends, met new people, had some hair-raising experiences like driving into Salta in Northern Argentina at midnight in a massive thunder storm when the streets were literally flowing like rivers and not knowing the location of our hotel! We thoroughly enjoyed it all. Long haul air travel has now lost its attraction and we concentrate today on holidays in Europe, where we can just as easily travel by rail rather than air, usually in greater comfort. The opening of the Channel Tunnel in 1992 and the development of links to an increasing number of European cities has promoted the scope for travel by train, thereby avoiding the aggravation invariably associated with passing through airports. We have indeed been lucky to have had such opportunities to travel to see the world.

Local activities have involved us both. Rosa still hunts and rides while for over twenty years she was a broderer at York Minster, part of a team of volunteers who work to provide the Minster and its clergy with their copes and chasubles, altar cloths, kneelers and other stitched accoutrements. It is skilled work and she has sewn since a very early age and loves it as well as being very accomplished. For my part I was elected in the mid-1990s as a freeman of the Company of Merchant Adventurers of the City of York, a well-known livery company with links to the Mercers Company in London and other sister mercantile companies of similar name in places like Bristol, Edinburgh and Richmond in North Yorkshire. Members are drawn from all parts of Yorkshire although in my time York seems to have become more predominant. The company's best-known event is the Venison Feast held at the beginning of November each year in the company's hall in Fossgate. Construction of the Merchant Adventurers' Hall, the oldest building in the city, began in 1357. I enjoy the various social occasions sponsored by the company and have twice sat on the Court, the committee of elected members who manage the charitable and other activities of the trust. Henry Woods, one of my predecessors in command of the Army in York proposed me for membership. I have never seen myself as a natural liveryman but have always been proud to have been involved alongside so many good friends in York and surrounding North and East Yorkshire.

I have shot all my life, a sporting activity I have always enjoyed but had to stop in 2006 when *cranial arteritis* led to my losing 90 per cent of the sight of my right eye, a loss for which there seemed to be no logical explanation. It was a great disappointment and I missed the camaraderie of the shoots where I took part but there was little to be done about that; maybe it was God's way of telling me it was time to put my gun away! People in Yorkshire were always very generous in their invitations. However, it was at Abernethy where I have shot most often and where I must have walked the moors and hills of the northern slopes of the Cairngorms for over sixty years, which gave me the greatest pleasure. My gun – a lovely 12 bore Holland and Holland given to me on my twenty-first birthday by my Uncle Hugh – now resides in the gun safe at Minster Hill but I hope one day a grandchild will be able to use it. Read a bit more about Abernethy towards the end of this book.

About twelve years ago I learnt to play bridge, a game I was originally introduced to behind the cricket pavilion at my prep school but had never played since! Virginia Storey, who lives nearby at Settrington, got a group of us together in 1998 to be instructed in the intricacies of the game and we all benefitted from what Peter Stocken, the President of the British Bridge Union and a contemporary of Virginia's husband Richard at Winchester, taught us. Peter, his wife and four children all play bridge at a rarefied level and one of his sons, Jack, now seems to have taught most people in Yorkshire. I think the bridge 'craze' has struck across the whole country in recent years and I am told more and more people are now playing. Be that as it may it is a great social game and, inter alia, helps to keep one's grey matter a bit sharper as old age and senility creep up but it can be tiresome if people take it too seriously! As time has gone by I have found myself playing in various groups – including with a coterie of male contemporaries playing in the winter months which I have organised now for ten years – and thoroughly enjoy it, despite making lots of mistakes, as indeed do others. Sadly, Rosa is yet to be persuaded to take up the game.

Huttons Ambo where we have now lived for nearly thirty years, is a delightful place lying as it does on the edge of Ryedale's Howardian Hills. Of course, it has changed in several ways over that time and no one would expect otherwise. There are now more young people living in the village than when we arrived, partly explained by the number of houses being rented out by the local estate owned by the Jenyns family. There is a welcome degree of socialising and the recent refurbishment of the village hall, some newly started activities, including the occasional Saturday lunch in the village hall and quizzes, have meant people come together more often than in the past. We are probably no different from other rural communities, although we are lucky to have a hard core of willing volunteers who work well as a team to bring people together. Long may it last!

About twenty-five years ago, Marcus Worsley (whom I met on the Canal du Midi in 1977), the Lord Lieutenant of North Yorkshire, invited me to become a Deputy Lieutenant for the county. It was an unexpected honour since I am not a Yorkshireman but, as I understand this particular system of representation at county level, retired service officers are particularly favoured as deputies to a lord lieutenant, whether because they are usually quite smart or because they can be trusted to organise events reasonably efficiently or because they may possess uniform, I am not sure. The duties, certainly in my time, were not onerous, most people preferring the lord lieutenant to attend an event rather than 'the organ grinder' although I believe one of Marcus's successors, Barry Dodd, changed the approach and DLs are now given rather more to do than was previously the case. Two events stick in my mind: the first when the Princess Royal came to Hunmanby to visit a Riding for the Disabled event and, because of the weather, her time of departure was brought forward necessitating my having to tell her to 'hurry up and finish what she was doing' whereupon she spoke to a large number of individuals in a very short space of time, a most professional and impressive performance. The second was a commemoration of the wartime land army when a series of tea parties was held across the county to celebrate the work of the land girls and the 'timber gills', those women who worked during the war years in forestry and sawmills. I hosted a reception for the latter at the Ryedale District Council Offices and it was very humbling to meet those who came and to listen to what they had to tell each other. I enjoyed my time as a DL but was always rather embarrassed at being appointed to the role; to me there seemed to be so many local people of distinction who had spent all their lives in the county and had made a great contribution to the North Yorkshire community who were just as deserving of the honour, if not more so.

Having reached well into my seventies and with less of an appetite for physical exercise – although I still try to keep myself fit mainly through walking when dogs provide important motivation to go out in all weathers – in 2011 I decided to turn my hand to further writing, principally for the pleasure it gave me. My love of all aspects of railways and an increasing respect for our medieval cathedral builders, engendered to an extent by my involvement at York Minster, determined me to try and link those two interests by travelling around England to describe what two groups of our ancestors – the Normans who built our early cathedrals, and later the Victorians who invented railways at the time of the Industrial Revolution – had bequeathed to those who followed them.

The underlying theme of both the books I subsequently wrote was to encourage readers to visit some of our great Anglican cathedrals and, in my second book, some of England's other great historic churches like our abbeys and minsters, and to do so as far as feasible by train. I felt it could be fairly argued that the Norman and Victorian eras were times of lasting discovery and development and I saw a connection between the two periods – separated as they were by eight hundred years of history – for the achievements of the people who lived in those times and for the enduring memorials they left to those who came later. Our Anglican cathedrals are, and always have been, jewels in the nation's crown, rightly celebrated for the magnificence of their architecture, their permanence as symbols of earlier times, the skills of their creators and the role they still play in promoting and sustaining the Anglican faith in Britain. Despite changing attitudes to religion and a decline in general church attendance, cathedrals still attract worshippers and visitors to their doors and have experienced something of a revival in recent years, judging by the increased numbers of both. I have always thought of them as one of the Britain's greatest heritages, on an entirely different plane with their neighbours on the Continent, both architecturally and in the welcome they provide to visitors.

Railways form a network of connections across the nation and there is no reason to assume that for the foreseeable future they will not continue to do so. Competing systems of transport like the motor car and the aeroplane play their part but, given the pressure for the nations of the world to take action to avoid the ravages of climate warming, they, as prominent consumers of fossil fuels, may soon pass into history to be replaced by more revolutionary transport alternatives such as electrical vehicles. A similar possibility may also await rail transport although efficient, economical and comfortable systems of travel, increasingly using electrical power, are always going to be needed. Both of my books set out to explain how the various cathedrals and other churches could be reached by rail and, in addition, included items of railway history and operations for those who might wish to understand more about today's railway system.

One of my aims in linking churches and trains was to highlight the principal points of interest to be found in the churches to be visited. People who go to great buildings or who may travel long distances are often unaware of what is to be seen or where they are passing. I wanted to ensure busy visitors and travellers with little time to spare would get full value for their time by being prepared for their visits and journeys. *England's Cathedrals by Train. Discover how the Normans and the Victorians helped to shape our lives*, was published by Pen & Sword Books of Barnsley in South Yorkshire in 2013 with a foreword written by Archbishop David Hope; *England's Historic Churches by Train. A Companion volume*, with a foreword by Bishop James Newcome, Bishop of Carlisle followed in 2016. Both books were seemingly well received with reasonable sales and I took a direct interest in promoting and selling both books, visiting many sales outlets myself.

Apart from setting down on paper in this book what I have done with my life I have no other plans to write again, despite people being kind enough to ask "when the next book is coming out?" Hours spent typing on a computer, the intense irritations that the Internet and its associated systems can impose and the time involved in correcting or redressing electronic interruptions have decided me that my foray into the world of authorship should best be closed. I love the written word but there must be a limit to how much of my writings should be inflicted on others!

Travel. Mount Cook, South Island, New Zealand 2012.

Travel. Hanoi, Vietnam 2000.

Travel. The Ravenna mosaics, Italy 2017.

Travel. Mount Washington rack railway, New Hampshire, USA 2010.

Trekking in Nepal 1999.
(Back l to r): Mike Hughes; Roger Preston; Charles Dawes; DMN; Bill Stanford; Mike Swindells.
(Front l to r): Val Dawes; Polly Preston, Sunamaya (Expedition host); Rosa Naylor.

The Paine Towers in Southern Chile.

Travel. The Igazu Falls, Argentina 2005.

Abernethy

I have already mentioned Abernethy on several occasions in this short history and it is indeed a place deserving of special mention for the pleasure it has given me, my siblings, my own immediate family and countless friends over many decades. In 2007, I put pen to paper to produce a very short booklet recounting the history of Abernethy in Inverness-shire and how the Naylors and, before them the Holts, came to be involved with the estate. That history, *Abernethy, a Diary and a Description*, summarises what has taken place there over many years and, if to hand, should be read in order to learn more about the place and why as a family we have endeavoured to preserve our links with that particular part of Scotland and still love it today.

Forest Lodge.

Very briefly my mother's family first visited the Northern Cairngorms area around the 1860s and in 1911 Richard Holt, my grandfather, took a sporting lease on Forest Lodge and the surrounding shooting and stalking grounds. Richard died in 1941 but my mother and father continued to rent the Lodge and the sporting from the Seafield family, the long-time owners. Twenty-five years later my father died and three years afterwards, Abernethy, along with a number of other Seafield owned properties bordering Strathspey and north towards the Moray Firth, were put up for sale heralding the virtual end of that family's land ownership in the area. As a consequence, in 1969 the Naylor family combined to purchase Forest Lodge and the surrounding high ground (but not the former lower ground shooting areas or any agricultural properties), owning it until 1988 when, for a number of reasons Christopher and I decided to divest ourselves of the place, selling the lodge and nearly all the land to the Royal Society for the Protection of Birds. The cost of running the estate, increasing environmental constraints and the fact that we were absentee landlords and unlikely ever to live there permanently, were all factors considered in our decision to sell.

On 31 March 1988, the RSPB acquired the property to allow the establishment of a reserve where species common to the Scottish Highlands might thrive under a management regime focussed principally on conservation. They were particularly keen to encourage capercaillie, black grouse, Scottish crossbills and crested tits inhabiting the forest and moorland areas, to flourish and Abernethy was promoted as a flagship project, growing in importance ever since.

Two particular aspects of our agreement with the RSPB worked in our favour: first it was accepted that Christopher and I should each continue to own a small house on the reserve – for him at Rynettin and for me at Lyngarrie – while it was also agreed that we and our families would be permitted to continue to shoot on some of the high ground grouse beats and also to stalk red deer, both activities we had undertaken in the past. It was an extraordinarily generous arrangement and has worked to perfection. We have made many good friends in the RSPB in the thirty years since the initial agreement was concluded and have all benefitted from being able to continue to visit and enjoy the place that Naylors have always loved and considered a second home. More recently my eldest son Nicholas and Christopher's daughter, Harriet, have negotiated an extension of the original agreement dating from 1988. I am not sure our neighbours on Speyside necessarily approved of our original decision to sell to the RSPB – sometimes rather crudely referred to as the 'bird people' – but as events have turned out I think we were possibly ahead of the times in doing so. Today the future of 'the Highland estate' is coming increasingly under the spotlight, not only for its role as a sporting enterprise but also for its position within a local community and its approach to land usage generally. Many criticisms of the existing order are manifestly unfair but I suspect some changes may be on the way.

On the hill with Christopher Clayton and the Parsons.

Lyngarrie.

With Desmond (RSPB former warden) and Morag Dugan at Lyngarrie.

At the end of a day.
Charles Dawes, Bill and Margaret Stanford and William.

Lyngarrie.

With Iain Ferguson at the Pass of Ryvoan.

I think the agreement with the RSPB is possibly unique. We have made it our business to support the local team and, in their turn, they have gone out of their way to accommodate us as much as that is possible, given the estate's changed role. Desmond Dugan, Stewart Taylor, Bob Moncrieff, and Jeremy Roberts and many others (there tends to be quite a turnover of staff although it is nice to able to record that many have settled locally in retirement) have all without exception, become and remain close friends. It is also good to see the Lodge – itself a fascinating building in that it is one of very few all wooden houses of such a large size in Britain – in the past shut up each winter – being used all the year round as the RSPB's office for the area. In addition to the former Abernethy estate the RSPB also manage other land holdings in Strathspey such as some of the high peaks in the Cairngorms, at Loch Garten with its long-established Osprey centre and some other smaller reserves.

For Christopher and me and our families to continue to able to go to Abernethy each year has been an enormous benefit and as a result our children and now our grandchildren have grown up to enjoy much the same outdoor life that we – and before us our parents' generation – also enjoyed. Shooting, stalking, climbing the hills, walking the wonderful pine forests, swimming in the lochs, fishing and discovering a host of other stimulating activities in places like Grantown or Aviemore have resulted in our going back year after year. We are indeed fortunate families thanks to the agreement made with the RSPB, and a determination by all of us to make the most of our opportunities. Over the years many friends have gone to Abernethy to enjoy the same pleasure we derive from being there which has of course been an added bonus.

Lyngarrie was originally a croft which was lived in by a shepherd and, more recently before its purchase by us, used by the Smith family, tenant farmers from Lurg. We converted it in 1986 to make a holiday home and it has been improved since then, mainly by Nicholas and Clare.

My memories of Abernethy now stretch back seventy years. During that time, I grew up in the shadow of Forest Lodge, mixing on closely supervised terms with my parents' friends, playing and discovering the joys of living in such a remote place and later tramping the hills with a gun or a rifle. It was an idyllic existence only marred when the time came to return to school, when tears were often shed! My mother adored Abernethy and could not conceive of spending her holidays anywhere else and I don't think I or my siblings would have disagreed with her when children! Thereafter, as we grew up, Christopher and I assumed more responsibility for running Abernethy, culminating in the time when we owned the estate and worked the woods for their timber. The sale to the RSPB changed much but has never altered our basic approach and it is a joy now to see children, grandchildren and their friends enjoying the place as much as we always did.

Sadly, many of the local people we got to know in our younger days have now died. Some like the Hamilton brothers, Bob Grant, Hamish Gordon and, when we owned Forest Lodge, Charlie Robertson, were all keepers or stalkers, but have now gone. Only Charlie at ninety-one remains. Contemplating former days and old friends can on occasions provoke sadness but the rapport we had with many people at Abernethy and the joy the place always gave us will remain with me for the rest of my life. In parallel with serving in the Scots Guards, my association with Abernethy has given me the greatest enjoyment of the last eighty years.

> *God gives all men Earth to love'*
> *But since man's heart is small,*
> *Ordains for each one spot shall prove*
> *Beloved over all.*

Rudyard Kipling (1865-1936)

Chieftain of the Abernethy Highland Games in 2016. With Neil Sutherland, Chairman of the games.

Chapter Six

An Ebbing Tide

Family

This may appear a rather sombre chapter heading for the last part of this book but it reflects the fact that I have now reached that stage in my life where ambition has begun to fade, physical ability is rather less than it used to be and my powers of recall are definitely less efficient than they were. That said I am still enjoying life and feel a sense of achievement at having now passed my eightieth year milestone with sufficient petrol still in the tank to travel further!

Peter's 90th Birthday. (l to r): Christopher; Carolyn; Peter; Mary-Anne and DMN.

This is the point at which to talk about my family. I have already written much about Rosa and the tremendous love and support she has always given me and I think there is little more to be said or done, other than to express immense gratitude. We have done lots of interesting things together, shared moments of joy and sadness, have enjoyed some wonderful experiences and have made a wide range of friends from many different walks of life in widely different parts of the world. I don't think I need say more.

Peter and Paddy at the Clockhouse.

Nicholas and Clare. Their wedding in August 1997.

I have generally remained on good terms with my siblings. Not surprisingly, we may not have always seen eye to eye but, between us, we have rubbed along pretty well, coming together when family matters had necessarily to take priority. This was particularly so when Christopher and I combined to manage Abernethy in the days when we owned the estate and the management of forestry operations demanded close consideration and careful financial understanding. Indeed, the handling of Abernethy and its subsequent successful sale to the RSPB in 1988 was led by Christopher and overall, he made the greatest contribution to our successful, if short-lived, stewardship of the estate.

Christopher worked most of his life in the shipping industry. He married Penelope Buxton in 1966 and they have two children – Tom and Harriet – and five grandchildren. Penelope and he now live at Ellesmere in Shropshire.

Carolyn married David Gardiner in 1963 and has lived practically all her wedded life on the Berkshire Downs north of Newbury. They have three children – James, Georgina and Andrew – and eight grandchildren. David started his working life in the family business of Huntley & Palmers of Reading which later became part of the Associated Biscuits group. Carolyn is a 'big shot' in the disabled riding world and recently became Chairman of the selection committee which picks those riders deemed suitable to represent Britain in the Para Olympic Games. She went to Rio de Janeiro in 2017.

Mary Anne lives near Port Laois in the Irish Republic. She married Oliver Onions in 1971 but, as recorded elsewhere, he died in 1985. They had two children – Mark and Roseanna – and Mary Anne now has five grandchildren. The Onions have long farmed in Co Laois, while Mary Anne is now heavily involved in stewarding at various race meetings in Ireland.

Half-brother Peter has already been mentioned and still lives at Far Sawrey in the Lake District. He has a son, Adam, married to Marianne, a granddaughter, Claire, and now two great grandchildren.

Nicholas, Clare, George and Daisy.

Peter and Rosa at the Clockhouse.

Once they set foot in the outside world life took each of my children in different directions and they all made their own decisions as to the careers they would like to follow; sadly, none included a service career although two of them contemplated 'joining up'; there were good reasons as to why they did not pursue that particular option but I believe that, had they joined one of the services, both Nicholas and William would have enjoyed the life and would have made a strong contribution.

Nicholas married Clare Jacobs in 1997 and, following a number of moves, they are now living at Yattendon in Berkshire close to where their two children, George and Daisy, are at school at Pangbourne College. Nicholas, a chartered accountant by profession, is at present the CEO of Allanby Capital, a City based firm advising and helping to grow businesses in the private and public sectors.

Hughie and Mary Blomfield live in Stoke Newington, North London and have three children, Meg, Kit and Ned, all of whom are being educated locally. Hughie is a qualified solicitor and, after service with some of the larger law firms in London, is now working with Trinity, a firm specialising in investment banking, creating wealth and value by advising clients, many of whom reside overseas. Mary trained as a midwife and currently works for the NHS as a health visitor in the East End of London.

William attended the Royal Agricultural College, Cirencester on leaving school, later graduating as a chartered surveyor. His early years were with Savills but, following a series of other moves, about ten years ago he established his own housing and letting business in Market Harborough, Leicestershire. He is married to Lis Welsh who has two daughters, Alex and Ellie, by a previous marriage. William and Lis live in the village of Tur Langton about six miles from Harborough. They have no children of their own. Lis is very entrepreneurial involving herself in a variety of undertakings; she is a talented artist, drawing and painting and enjoys sculpture. There's not much she seemingly cannot turn her hand to!

An enormous and recent joy for me was when the three boys arranged an eightieth birthday party for me in London to which they asked a number of my old friends and their own immediate families. On that occasion we were surrounded by people who are and always have been real friends, people who make life worthwhile and who would I know always come to our assistance should that be necessary. I am very proud of how the boys, their wives and our grandchildren conduct themselves. Rosa and I are indeed fortunate.

Hughie graduating from Southampton.

Mary at Abernethy.

Ned, Kit and Hughie.

Rosa with Meg and Kit.

Willie and Lis on Exmoor.

Reflections

Inevitably I have seen many changes in my life but equally so will have most other people. Changes in political, social and behavioural attitudes, developments in technology, scope for wider travel and the chance to learn about other people inhabiting the globe and, maybe perhaps most significantly, changes to the notion of what the term family means in the second decade of the twenty-first century, have all had an influence on me and those around me. I don't think it is necessary to go into any of the above in detail other than to comment that change in the way life is led is constant and, whether one approves or not, most developments are usually for the best even if one disagrees at the time. However, there are some facets of life which are deserving of mention because of the impact they have had on me in a more personal sense.

I think we live in a fairer world than when I was born. Although differentials in wealth and possessions still exist and probably always will, we are generally more tolerant in our attitudes; as a pensioner I feel that I have been well looked after by successive governments and have been justly rewarded for a life as a serviceman. Whether the same will be true for future generations as the nation's economy fluctuates to reflect political and strategic variations in a world where many countries seem to be in a state of almost continual turmoil, I cannot tell and, looking to the future, I sometimes fear where the years ahead will lead for future generations. Internal politics in Britain have never been more fragmented and it is hard to see where our political parties may find themselves in the future, while Brexit, the outcome of which will decide the nation's course for many years ahead, remains a sword of Damocles poised over us all without our having any real knowledge of what is to come or what is best for Britain. All that said, the threat of major change accompanied by auguries of potential disaster have been encountered before and have usually been survived.

More worrying is the nation's apparent inability to find people of calibre and integrity to lead the country. Often in my lifetime Britain has been led by people of great stature who were able to guide the country through some dark periods in our history, people who were prepared to set aside political differences for the common good, uniting us in doing so. Sadly, today there seem few real leaders in society prepared to raise their sights above the level of petty party prejudices and able to give a realistic moral lead on issues of great complexity. Eighty years ago, Winston Churchill was about to lead the nation through six years of global conflict, soldiers like Montgomery and Slim were instrumental in motivating defeated armies to win great battles, while later prime ministers like Margaret Thatcher and others cajoled the nation into getting a grip when required. Where are their equivalents today?

Further afield, the rise of China, the instability of America under President Trump including the bombast displayed in his dealings with North Korea, the ISIS jihadists and their poisonous doctrines and the increasingly bellicose attitudes being struck by the Russian Federation, are all of enormous concern. I suspect many people believe 'hot' wars between nations to be a thing of the past and that an attempt by one nation to subjugate another is more likely to be attempted by means other than armed combat including a range of electronic measures designed to cripple vital civilian services or by the restricting of energy supplies or critical raw materials in order to immobilise an adversary. I am not so sure and believe there is little room for such complacent thinking. We need only look at the Crimea and Ukraine and the hostile attitudes recently struck by the Russian Federation in its determination to restore to its people some of the influence and power which the USSR lost in the last years of the twentieth century. An attack on the west by Russia, while currently unlikely, conjures up a horrifying prospect. While I still have faith in many of those who guide the affairs of this nation, the diplomatic voice of Britain is today very soft, an unpalatable indication of how low the nation's influence on world affairs has sunk. Above all we should remember that deep down Hitler's motive for beginning the Second World War was to provide greater living space for the German people for their economic benefit; what might be President Putin's calculation in doing something similar to restore to his people a feeling of lost national pride?

The creation of the internet and a wide range of communication ancillaries has certainly helped businesses, service industries, government, local authorities and individuals to make quicker and more efficient contact with one another and of course we now find we cannot do without such technology. Systems under the general heading of computing are, and always have been, very much a younger person's province. My grandchildren are probably more proficient than their parents and the latter are certainly light years ahead of me in getting the best out of modern devices. However, in the thirty or so years I have used a computer I have endured more frustration and irritation than in any other sphere of my life, most of it caused by the operating vagaries of provider systems and those who purport to manage them. In my experience one of the most frequent challenges faced is to identify the right person or people to help one in a crisis. I cannot believe my parents faced the same challenges when telephones first made an appearance! I am not on Facebook or Twitter or any other social media and don't wish to be, despite the admonitions I frequently receive about as a result being left behind. It is not therefore for me to comment upon the effects of social media, but by all accounts, they can have malign side effects which all too easily cause psychological damage to individual users. Young people are especially vulnerable while 'hacking' can affect us all and is entirely unselective in its application. I cannot help but feel that the internet in all its many forms may well eventually breed a race of automatons.

To my mind the world now contains far too many people and ever-growing populations, particularly in the more undeveloped parts of the globe, threaten strife and bloodshed. Given the tensions between the 'global powers' and elsewhere, a propensity for people threatened by famine, religious intolerance and racial differences to move at will to seek pastures new, the next decades are going to see more friction and displacement than has occurred since the beginning of the twenty-first century. The world is becoming inherently unstable.

Man is a selfish creature, often unthinking and destructive in his attitudes. His ignorance of the natural environment, the squandering of diminishing resources and his disregard for the feelings of others are well known and apply to the great majority of us, myself included. Society is intolerant of interference in its pleasures and the way we treat, for example, dwindling numbers of wonderful wildlife and the advantage we take of domestic creatures, particularly food animals when the tolerance of religious taboos can impose unacceptable suffering, sometimes borders on the barbaric. Of course, we need to eat to live but the sometimes callous rearing of sentient creatures should shame us. Humans are not always as compassionate as they like to pretend.

An oft used excuse regularly heard is 'what can I do on my own to rectify some of the abuses currently practiced by mankind'. The short answer is probably very little although on those occasions when we do band together, we can often achieve a disproportionate result; while finding some pressure groups irritating and irrational, it has to be said that a number of those which have arisen over recent years have had a beneficial effect in redressing wrongs or drawing attention to fundamentally unfair or unsafe practices. David Attenborough's recent programmes on the oceans and the dangers of mindless waste disposal are a good example. He and others are to be applauded.

However, we should not forget that the British are, generally speaking, a fair minded and tolerant people, and I for one have been proud to have been born a Briton. A parliamentary democracy, a system of law administered by some of the country's best legal minds, armed forces whose loyalty has never occasioned them to try to subvert a popularly elected government and a media which, although often driven by its own practices to unacceptable excesses, still enshrines valuable standards of reporting, are all institutions vital to the well-being of the British people. We allow any of them to be jeopardized at our peril.

One aspect of life which I have always held dear is that I live in a nation comprised of four quite different but closely linked countries, each speaking the same language. To be able to say that one lives in the United Kingdom, made up of England, Scotland, Wales and Northern Ireland, is a source of immense pride to me. As a nation we are united by far more than the issues which from time to time may divide us and I for one hope that recent attempts to break up the kingdom, if repeated, will not succeed. Too much would be at stake, not least the strength we derive from being united, and I have little doubt that succeeding generations would come to regret such a move. So there it is: I count myself to be a loyal citizen in the best sovereign nation in the world, overseen by the most dignified and upstanding monarch of all time; the privilege to live in a beautiful natural environment, a belief in a Christian faith, generally good health, supportive friends and a wonderful family. Nobody could wish for more. I am indeed a fortunate man and always have been.

Epilogue

Histories generally reflect people because people are what make life interesting. This autobiography is no exception and I have tried to include as many names as possible. In general, those mentioned are people I have worked with or alongside both as a soldier and more recently in retirement. For reasons of space I have not been able to include the names of many of those people met in the course of everyday life or socially, all of whom are just as important to me and whose friendships mean just as much as those whose names are recorded. Lack of mention should not be assumed to be a lack of interest.

Bibliography

The Family of Naylor from 1589 by Thomas Naylor. Printed by Tinlings of Liverpool 1967 and released by Dorothy. I.D.Naylor 1967.

Among Friends, The Scots Guards 1956 – 1993 by Murray Naylor. Published 1995 by Leo Cooper, 190 Shaftesbury Avenue, London WC2H 8JL.

Index to names

This book contains a large number of names but, as a general rule, only those who appear twice or more in the text are recorded in the index. In addition, ranks and titles are not given since many of the names mentioned in the book have held different ranks or titles at different times.

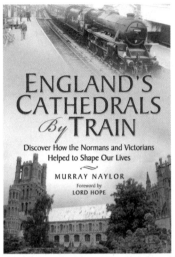

England's Cathedrals By Train
Murray Naylor

One of the jewels in the nation's crown is its Anglican cathedrals. Many, constructed after the invasion of 1066, stand as monuments to the determination and commitment of their Norman builders. Others have been built in later centuries while some started life as parish churches and were subsequently raised to cathedral status. Places of wonder and beauty, they symbolize the Christian life of the nation and are more visited today than ever as places which represent England's religious creed, heritage and the skills of their builders. Eight hundred years later came the Victorians who pioneered the Industrial Revolution and created railways. Like their Norman predecessors they built to last and the railway system bequeathed to later generations, has endured in much the same form as when originally constructed. There is little sign that railways will be displaced by other modes of transport, anyway in the foreseeable future, Combining a study of thirty-three English cathedrals and the railway systems which allow them to be reached, the author seeks to celebrate these two magnificent institutions. In the process he hopes to encourage others to travel the same journeys as he himself has undertaken.

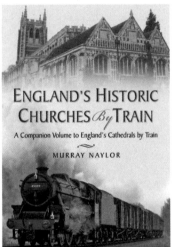

England's Historic Churches By Train
Murray Naylor

Travelling across England it selects thirty-two of our ancient churches, relating their history and identifying those aspects which a visitor might overlook. His journeys include the great medieval abbeys at Tewkesbury, Selby and Hexham; the less well known priories at Cartmel and Great Malvern and other grand churches severely reduced after the Dissolution of Henry VIII s reign, notably at Bridlington and Christchurch. He visits a church at Chesterfield where the spire leans at a crooked angle and goes to Boston, where the church - known as the Stump was a starting point for many who emigrated to America in the 17th Century. In describing his journeys by train the author includes information appropriate to individual routes and incorporates topics of railway interest relevant to the development and management of todays railway systems. He does so in a manner similar to that adopted in his previous books on cathedrals.

Murray Naylor sells both books himself and can be contacted as follows:
(a) by email: murray.naylor64@gmail.com or (b) by telephone 07889138381 or (c) by mail to Minster Hill, Huttons Ambo, York. YO60 7HJ.

Details of both books can be viewed on the Pen and Sword Books website from whom books can also be purchased.